# Contents

# Portrait of a Gallery

**THESCOTTISHGALLERY**

CONTEMPORARY ART SINCE 1842

16 Dundas Street, Edinburgh, EH3 6HZ  |  +44 (0)131 558 1200  |  mail@scottish-gallery.co.uk  |  scottish-gallery.co.uk

1842 1843 1844 1845 1846 1847 1848 1849 1850 1851 1852 1853 1854 1855 1856 1857 1858 1859 1860 1861 1862 1863 1864 1865 1866 1867 1868 1869 1870 1871 1872 1873 1874 1875 1876 1877 1878 1879 1880 1881 1882 1883 1884 1885 1886 1887 1888 1889 1890 1891 1892 1893 1894 1895 1896 1897 1898 1899 1900 1901 1902 1903 1904 1905 1906 1907 1908 1909 1910 1911 1912 1913 1914 1915 1916 1917 1918 1919 1920 1921 1922 1923 1924 1925 1926 1927 1928 1929 1930 1931 1932 1933 1934 1935 1936 1937 1938 1939 1940 1941 1942 1943 1944 1945 1946 1947 1948 1949 1950 1951 1952 1953 1954 1955 1956 1957 1958 1959 1960 1961 1962 1963 1964 1965 1966 1967 1968 1969 1970 1971 1972 1973 1974 1975 1976 1977 1978 1979 1980 1981 1982 1983 1984 1985 1986 1987 1988 1989 1990 1991 1992 1993 1994 1995 1996 1997 1998 1999 2000 2001 2002 2003 2004 2005 2006 2007 2008 2009 2010 2011 2012 2013 2014 2015 2016 2017

175 YEARS OF ART

/ ONE /

# Portrait of a Gallery

8

# Portrait of a Gallery

'The Scottish Gallery celebrates 175 years of art in 2017. The Scottish Gallery is the oldest privately owned, commercial gallery in Scotland and 175 years of continuous trading is an astonishing achievement for a small company. The Gallery is a living record and reflection of artistic and cultural evolution in Scotland whilst our emphasis is on the present and future as an ambassador for creative talent from Scotland.' — Will Whitehorn, Chairman

**A work of art is likely to outlast its maker and its first owner is also a custodian, each transaction the start of a journey, the life of objects informing the lives of humans. So, in this catalogue and exhibition we can celebrate the old that was once new and the new that will become old, the close relationships between gallery and artist and between collector, gallery and artist, while keeping our face turned resolutely forward.**

An art gallery has no order book, and the emphasis in planning must always be the future, immediate and near. A balance needs to be achieved to both reflect taste and lead it, to support new art and ideas as well as supply an art market. A work of art is likely to outlast its maker, and its first owner is also a custodian, each transaction the start of a journey, the lives of objects informing the lives of humans. So, in this catalogue and exhibition we can celebrate the old that was once new and the new that will become old, the close relationships between gallery and artist and between collector, gallery and artist, while keeping our face turned resolutely forward.

Aitken Dott was one of four children, born in 1815 in Cupar, where he was brought up. The name was Huguenot in origin and Dott's grandfather had worked as a sculptor on the University of Edinburgh's Old College Quad in 1789. How Dott came to found a firm of 'Gilders, Framers and Artists' Colourmen' in May 1842 is not known, but we can imagine the entrepreneurial spirit he must have needed. Edinburgh was still a city of Enlightenment in the 1840s, home to writers, philosophers, publishers and entrepreneurs, and to painters able to train at the Trustees Academy, develop a portrait practice without the necessity of moving to London and exhibit their work in the Royal Scottish Academy, founded in 1826. Artists began to exhibit independently of their patrons and required galleries and exhibitions in which to display their paintings for sale.

Previous: The Scottish Gallery window display at 26 South Castle Sreet, c.1951

Opposite: Aitken Dott by Robert McGregor, 1891. National Galleries Scotland

The business thrived, and in 1860 new, larger premises were occupied at 26 South Castle Street, which would be occupied for the next 120 years. It is likely that the move was driven by a desire for more hanging space, but it was not until 1897 that The Scottish Gallery was given its name and became almost a separate business within Aitken Dott & Son. The son was Peter McOmish Dott, who was born in 1856. He and his brother, Langair, became partners, but McOmish Dott was the more able and interested and by 1900 was the sole proprietor. McOmish Dott was a good businessman and an enlightened employer, devising a profit-sharing scheme for the employees and ensuring that the reputation of the firm grew and became a byword for quality. He was also a connoisseur with tremendous knowledge of painting and aesthetics. It was his idea to create The Scottish Gallery to differentiate picture dealing from the other parts of the business. The event was published in *The Art Journal* in 1897:

'…a new gallery has just been opened in Edinburgh, called The Scottish Gallery, avowedly and specially for the exhibition of works of Scottish painters. Messrs. Dott & Co., the young partners of a house long honourably known in the North, brought together in the past autumn a collection of 200 excellent examples of the best artists in Scotland and the reception the collection met ensures that it will be followed by others in the same character.'

The article goes on to highlight works by W.D. Mackay, Hugh Cameron, Sam Bough, William McTaggart and James Lawton Wingate. McOmish Dott was a tremendous advocate of McTaggart, writing a learned introduction to his major exhibition of 1907, which celebrated fifty years of association with The Gallery.

He also oversaw a programme of regular one-person exhibitions of work by new painters. The Gallery was still only one part of a larger business and the partners had options about how to use it: for S.J. Peploe's first one-person show in 1903 the gallery was rented to the artist who was responsible for all the costs and arrangements in return for a small (ten per cent) commission. In 1908, perhaps recognising the need to modernise, McOmish Dott took on a younger partner, George Proudfoot, and they together undertook a major refurbishment of the premises, creating the splendid first-floor galleries at number 26.

Opposite: The Scottish Gallery at 26 South Castle Street, c.1940s.
© Crown Copyright: Historic Environment Scotland

"....a new gallery has just been opened in Edinburgh, called The Scottish Gallery, avowedly and specially for the exhibition of works of Scottish painters. Messrs. Dott & Co., the young partners of a house long honourably known in the North, brought together in the past autumn a collection of 200 excellent examples of the best artists in Scotland and the reception the collection met ensures that it will be followed by others in the same character."

22357
TELEPHONE: CENTRAL 2157.
TELEGRAMS: PICTURES, EDINBURGH.

ESTABLISHED 1842
AITKEN DOTT & SON,
DEALERS IN FINE PICTURES & ETCHINGS.

THE SCOTTISH GALLERY,
26 CASTLE STREET,
EDINBURGH.

J. W. Blyth. Esq.
Wiltz House
Kirkcaldy

| 1945 | | | | |
|---|---|---|---|---|
| Oct. 23 | To water colour 'A Street in Cairo' by Sir D.Y. Cameron. | 18 | · | · |
| 31 | " 'Still Life', by Duncan Grant | 112 | · | · |
| | " 'Barra', small oil by S.J. Peploe. R.S.A. | 80 | · | · |
| Nov. 30 | " water colour, 'Black bird on Branch' by Edwin Alexander. R.S.A. | 60 | · | · |
| | " 2 small Pictures — Coast Scene, by Wm W. Taggart R.S.A. & 'Wind', by S.J. Peploe. R.S.A. | 60 | · | · |
| 1946 | | 330 | · | · |
| Feby. | By 'Iona', by S.J. Peploe. R.S.A. | 100 | · | · |
| | | 230 | · | · |
| 45 Nov. | To Frame Dept a/c :— To finishing frame in toned bronze new back & fitting Picture by David Muirhead. | 1 | · | · |
| 46 Feby. 12. | " Glass & 3 ply back & refitting Picture by Duncan Grant 24 × 20 | — | 12 | 6 |
| | £ | 231 | 12 | 6 |

Above: Invoice from Aitken Dott & Son, The Scottish Gallery to J.W. Blyth, 1940
Opposite: Invoice from Aitken Dott & Son, The Scottish Gallery to J.W. Blyth, 1945–46

John Waldegrave Blyth (1873–1962) was a Kirkcaldy linen manufacturer with a passion for art that began in his early thirties. By the time of his death he had amassed a collection of 237 works including 84 by S.J. Peploe. Much of his collection was sourced from The Scottish Gallery, his first McTaggart acquired in 1910. His passion for art extended into direct advocacy as he organised a show of Scottish Art at the Royal Academy in 1939. He was a Trustee of The National Galleries of Scotland after the War and much of his collection eventually came to Kirkcaldy Museum and Art Gallery.

Above: S.J. Peploe and his students,
Edinburgh College of Art, 1934

Opposite: S.J. Peploe, *Still Life with Bottle*, c.1913,
oil on canvas, 51 x 51 cms. Exhibited: The Scottish Gallery,
Edinburgh, early 1920s; *S.J. Peploe, Scotland's First Modernist*,
The Scottish Gallery, 2012, cat. 16. Sold by The Gallery, 2012

This painting, which we can date to c.1913, is one of a small
group of cubist-influenced works made in Paris and Edinburgh
before the First World War. There had been the promise
and expectation of an exhibition of new work at The Scottish
Gallery when Peploe left for Paris in the spring of 1910, but
the expressionist Royan and Paris panels and a few 'modernist'
still-life pieces such as this example were too great a change
for McOmish Dott and the show was hastily rearranged for
the New Gallery in Shandwick Place, the home of the Society
of Eight. Within a year or so, Dott had retired and his younger
partner George Proudfout re-established an exhibiting
relationship with Peploe.

It was a time of transition in many ways. A generation
of landscape and genre painters, mostly senior
academicians, had been represented by The Gallery,
but by 1910 younger artists, trained in Paris,
were demanding attention as the inspiration of
Post-Impressionism worked its way through the
institutions and consciousness of the art establishment
and public.

The change in Scotland is best illustrated by The
Scottish Gallery's relationship with Samuel John Peploe
(1871–1935). As we have noted, he had his first show
in 1903, comprising impressionist landscapes, still lifes
and figure compositions painted in a fluid manner that
recalls both Whistler and Manet. The show was a
success and he showed again in 1909, in a similar vein,
though he now pushed the limits of this early technical
mastery in interiors with his new model, Peggy McRae.
But the show was also something of a clear-out; he
had decided to move to Paris, partly at the urging of
his friend John Duncan Fergusson. The winds of change
were upon him and within two years he saw his earlier
work with a sort of disdain – brilliant but limited. The
work he brought back to show McOmish Dott in 1911
horrified the senior partner – brilliantly coloured panels
of Royan and Brittany and the Paris parks and a few still
lifes in a Van Gogh style. Initially rejected by The Gallery,
Peploe showed his work in London with the Baillie and
Stafford Galleries, and he put on his own show in the
New Galleries in Shandwick Place, home of the artist-
run Society of Eight. Dott retired shortly afterwards and
George Proudfoot quietly mended the fences, buying
work during the war years and overseeing one-man
shows in 1922, 1925, 1927 and 1930.

George Proudfoot became a tremendous advocate for
the next generation of artists. In the 1920s, Dotts, in

conjunction with Alex. Reid & Lefevre, had contracts with both Peploe and
Leslie Hunter based on guarantees to purchase paintings (in the case of Hunter,
£600 a year). Proudfoot and Duncan MacDonald of Alex. Reid's would come
to the studio and, buying jointly, would take alternating picks, reflecting both
Glasgow and Edinburgh tastes, while as his wife recalled
'Sam would go for a walk'.

The other passion of Proudfoot was the work of a
generation of brilliant British etchers, whose popularity
in the twenties constituted a golden age for the medium.
Seymour Hayden, Edmund Blampied, the Swede Anders
Zorn and the Scots D.Y. Cameron, James McBey and
Muirhead Bone figured most prominently. The public
rooms of the shipping line owner Major Ion Harrison's
home in Helensburgh was sumptuously hung with the
work of Peploe, Hunter and F.C.B. Cadell, but the stairs
were full of the latest, most sought-after prints by
these masters. The print department, at various stages
encompassing master reproductions, etchings and an
antiquarian department, was a feature of The Gallery
up until the 1980s. In more recent times, when artists
like Elizabeth Blackadder and Victoria Crowe have made
printmaking a significant part of their creative output,
The Gallery has recognised this with exhibitions. In
addition, there have been significant exhibitions of
individual major printmakers, such as the first Howard
Hodgkin show in Scotland, which was at the art fair held
at Edinburgh College of Art in 1985.

In the post-war decades The Gallery fostered the
careers of the painters who formed the Edinburgh
School, and in particular William Gillies. George Proudfoot gave way first to
his sister, the redoubtable Miss Proudfoot, and then his young French widow,
who also looked after his significant personal collection. Gillies died in 1973
and by then The Gallery had sold well over 1,000 works for him, more than
half to the collector Robert Lillie, the pick of whose collection eventually went
to The Scottish National Gallery of Modern Art. In this sense, a significant

Joan Eardley sketching on the
street, Townhead, c.1950.
Photo: Audrey Walker

# JOAN EARDLEY
## RSA (1921–1963)

The Macaulay Children, c.1957, oil on board, 60 x 37.5, 80, 37.5 cms (3 panels)
Provenance: Private collection, Edinburgh
From left to right: Madeleine, Amanda, Andrew, Martin, John

This work, the only known commissioned painting by the artist, has as its subject
the five children of William Macaulay and his wife, a daughter of Sir David Russell
of Markinch and Iona. Neither the artist nor the children were enthusiastic about
the sittings, and its outcome is a tribute to Eardley's regard for Bill Macaulay,
the senior partner of The Scottish Gallery and her gentle guide through the
commercial art world. She tried hard and has made in the end a successful work,
capturing the children full of mischief and character. A great many preparatory
sketches and drawings were required and sometimes appear on the market
confused as Townhead street children.

WEEKEND

## Portrait of a gallery

RUTH WISHART CELEBRATES THE 150th ANNIVERSARY OF SCOTLAND'S FINEST ART DEALERS

The Scotsman, Saturday, May 30, 1992

ESTABLISHED 1842
*Fine Art Dealers*
94 GEORGE STREET
EDINBURGH EH2 3DF

*The Scottish Gallery.*
*127ᵃ George Street,*
*Edinburgh,*

portion of the modern collection was acquired indirectly through The Scottish Gallery, and many other inspired purchases of work by artists as diverse as Joan Eardley, William Gear, Robin Philipson and Rory McEwan came into the National Collection from The Gallery. The career of Philipson, Gillies' successor as Head of the School of Drawing and Painting, blossomed under the guidance of Bill Macaulay, the gentle academic who steered the business through the confusions of the sixties and seventies. By the mid seventies, Bill Jackson was at the helm and Guy Peploe joined him in late 1983. There were major shows of new work during the Edinburgh International Festival for John Bellany in 1985, Bruce McLean (including a performance which took place at the Fruitmarket Gallery) in 1986 and important survey exhibitions exploring the theme of modernism in Scottish painting throughout the decade. The eighties also saw the huge expansion of the art fair, and The Gallery participated in yearly events in London and Bath, as well as forays to Basel, Chicago, Los Angeles, and Madrid. It was an exciting time for painting that saw the emergence of the New Glasgow Group, including the prodigious talents of Stephen Conroy and Alison Watt, who had her first major solo show in The Gallery's short-lived London premises in 1990.

The Gallery finally moved from South Castle Street in 1981; a short move to 94 George Street, premises with a narrow Victorian shop front and a splendid gallery under a wide rectangular cupola. The shop was initially occupied with artist's materials in a franchise arrangement with Miller's Graphics, before an award-winning conversion was commissioned to accommodate an exhibition programme for objects. This was not out of the blue: The Gallery had always shown objects, including a Cartier jewellery exhibition in 1914. When an

Opposite, clockwise from top:

Bruce McLean Dinner, Festival 1986

*Portrait of A Gallery*, article by Ruth Wishart, The Scotsman, May 1992

Archive images, 1970s and 80s

Quality in art is not subject to fashionable shifts beyond the vagaries of the marketplace (which as market insiders we seek to exploit in any case) and it is to this we cleave in all our planning. In this we have a huge resource in our own history and are delighted to rediscover artists from our past, rekindle and celebrate many of the trade relationships we have enjoyed before and highlight some of the stories which lend colour and humanity to the process of display and sale which is still the business of The Scottish Gallery.

Opposite: Cat.1, Bruce McLean, Untitled, c.1989. screenprint, 156 x 106 cms, edition 9/30

artist like Jessie M. King decorated pots or Anne Redpath painted furniture or Alan Davie designed jewellery, The Gallery exhibited the work. In the post-war decades The Gallery reflected the fruitful relationship between artist and manufacture, showing, for example, the ceramics of Eduardo Paolozzi and then Bruce McLean. Henry Rothschild of the Primavera Gallery put on two brilliant survey exhibitions of British and European studio pottery, including Lucie Rie and Hans Coper, and many makers were represented in our regular summer and Christmas exhibitions. But the commitment was now substantial and Amanda Game was recruited in 1987 to take the policy forward. The touring exhibition *Shape and Surface*, curated by Joan Crossley-Holland of the former Oxford Gallery, included work by many major figures who are still represented today, including jewellers Wendy Ramshaw and Jacqueline Mina and ceramicists Alan Caiger-Smith, Gordon Baldwin, Sutton Taylor and Takeshi Yasuda. Today the departmental nature of the business has subsided in favour of a more integrated approach which incorporates design, the decorative and fine arts. Our commitment to the very best of international objects is undimmed, and is upheld both in The Gallery in Dundas Street, with ground-breaking exhibitions and participation in national and international Art Fairs.

The nineties were a time of consolidation after the recession of 1990, which briefly threatened the future of The Gallery as we disposed of our London business. It was a time that also saw the rebuilding of relationships with senior Scottish painters such as John Houston, Elizabeth Blackadder and David Michie, the emergence of Barbara Rae as a great colourist and the late flowering of the career of Alberto Morrocco. The Gallery became a consistent and successful exhibitor in the two most important London art fairs, Islington and the Royal College, where we were able to extend the market and reputation of our gallery artists. In this century we have seen an atomized art world, the failure of the predicted death of painting (while conceptual art dominates the establishment) and the revival of connoisseurship. All this in a period of very rapid growth followed by a decade of credit crunch, the vicissitudes of the wider economy and politics smoothed out by good forward planning, fiscal caution and artistic bravery.

In this period, The Gallery has invested in the space overseeing a complete physical upgrading of our Georgian rooms to balance the requirement to display both historic and contemporary work. Today the visitor will discover the beautiful spaces over two floors including our sculpture garden, transformed each month to display our exhibition programme. Post 2008, The Directors saw opportunities to invest in our history mounting major exhibitions, for example of The Roberts, William Johnstone, William Crosbie and exhaustive survey shows, as well as our Modern Masters series, each with ambitious publications. Our adherence to original and effective design across digital and print, using photography and archive images in conjunction with talented designers has enabled us to raise our profile for both The Gallery and the artists we represent. At the same time, we have sought to add to our contemporary field and have introduced photography in the shape of the international image maker, curator and director David Eustace. We have also formed productive partnerships with the St Judes artists and in our 175th anniversary year, we designed a programme of exhibitions reflecting past, present and future artists which most importantly introduced many new artists to The Gallery. The Scottish Gallery seeks to cover all territory while maintaining a unified attitude to quality and potential embodied by Christina Jansen, the Managing Director as well as Tommy Zyw, Guy Peploe and a talented staff.

In this publication we celebrate a long and diverse history, sharing stories that help illuminate all the art we have displayed and sold over the decades. We cannot attempt to include everything and so must issue a blanket apology for all the omissions, of which there are far more than inclusions. Our history reflects the taste of dozens of men and women who have worked here. Our brilliant artists and dedicated staff will continue to guarantee more wonderful art and reasons to love The Scottish Gallery.

The Scottish Gallery,
March 2017

22

# TWO

# A Landscape Tradition

# A Landscape Tradition

Three artists perhaps should be singled out for the parts they played in establishing the iconography and characteristics of what most people would recognise as archetypal Scottish landscapes. In 1840, two years before the founding of Aitken Dott's business, the man described by the great Sir David Wilkie as the 'founder of the landscape school of Scotland', Alexander Nasmyth, died aged eighty-two. He is particularly noted for his large panoramic Scottish landscapes and townscapes characterised by topographical correctness and attention to detail. Initially these have a strong sense of the picturesque inspired by works seen on an extended trip to Italy in the 1780s. Later his work changed, possibly under the influence of Dutch landscapes, and a broader, more atmospheric approach is also evident. In the late 1780s he opened a school for landscape painting in Edinburgh, which placed great emphasis on drawing trips to promote direct observation of the natural landscape.

**The landscape painter may well return to the same subject, in its infinite variety over a lifetime but may also seek new inspiration with travel.**

In the same year another important but younger figure also died. The Rev. John Thomson of Duddingston had indeed taken some lessons from Nasmyth, but was largely self-taught and developed into a painter of free brushwork and dramatic compositions in which Highland Scotland was seen as a place of wildness of nature often punctuated with built reminders of its turbulent history. Thomson was a true Romantic in his approach to painting and it is certain that no small influence was his long-term friendship with novelist and poet Sir Walter Scott, that great promoter of the romance of Scottish history and of national identity. Scott's atmospheric descriptions of the Scottish landscape used for poetic or narrative effect surely find parallels in Thomson's own heightened sense of the dramatic.

Horatio McCulloch (1805–1867) was very much an Aitken Dott artist and perhaps more than any other helped create the nineteenth-century image of the Scottish Highlands. His work is based on many painting trips to the Highlands, Skye and the Western Isles, during which he produced lively watercolours and oil sketches which were later worked up into larger, freely painted works in the studio. His hugely popular portrayal of the Scottish landscape was further disseminated through the many popular engravings made after his paintings.

Previous: Arthur Melville, Hillside, Invertrossachs, 1893, watercolour, 37 x 54 cms (detail) (cat.5)

**DUNCAN SHANKS**
**RSA, RSW (b.1937)**

Cat.2, River Moon, 2017, acrylic
on paper, 89 x 71 cms. Exhibited:
*Duncan Shanks, Winter Journey*,
The Scottish Gallery, Edinburgh,
cat.13, 2017

Our first comprehensive sales records date from the inaugural Scottish Gallery exhibition in 1896, in which works were shown by a range of well-established and younger artists (much as The Gallery does today), many of them landscape specialists. These included artists from all over Scotland, such as Hugh Cameron, W.D. McKay, Lawton Wingate, Robert McGregor and Robert Noble from Edinburgh, the Glasgow painters Alexander Roche, J. Morris Henderson and Archibald Kay, and from the south-west W.S. McGeorge and Bessie MacNicol. The inclusion of works by deceased artists like Sam Bough and Horatio McCulloch reveals the continuation of a well-established pattern of dealing in earlier works, bought back, reconsigned or acquired from auction rooms.

The landscape painter may well return to the same subject in its infinite variety over a lifetime, but may also seek new inspiration with travel. William McTaggart (1835–1910) began as a genre painter and finished as an impressionist concerned chiefly with landscape (of Argyll, Kintyre, the Angus coast, Forth estuary and Midlothian). He was prolific and ambitious and painted in oil and watercolour in both minute and monumental scale. His commercial relationship with The Scottish Gallery was of paramount importance to both for over fifty years. Even during the Second World War, his paintings, glazed and in magnificent swept and gilded frames, hung on the staircase at 26 South Castle Street, and had to be removed to safety overnight for fear of German bombing. Peploe, Hunter and Cadell, who are covered in chapter three, all worked in landscape. McTaggart and Gillies (both before and after the war) and then Dawyck Haig, consistently from 1945 until his death in 2008, John Houston, James Morrison and Duncan Shanks have all breathed new life and impetus into the landscape genre through their exhibitions with The Scottish Gallery; likewise with James Cowie, Joan Eardley, Robert Henderson Blyth, David Donaldson, John Gardiner Crawford, Barbara Rae, Jock McFadyen, Philip Braham and so on. Without a doubt, the landscape tradition is rich and the future optimistic.

## WILLIAM MCTAGGART
## RSA, RSW (1835–1910)

Opposite: The Preaching of St Columba,
1895, oil on canvas, 51 x 63.5 cms.
Sold by the Gallery, 2016

Right: Cat.3, Autumn Showers, 1891, oil on panel,
18 x 27 cms. Exhibited: *Modern Masters VI*,
The Scottish Gallery, Edinburgh, 2017, cat.7.
Provenance: Private collection, Tomintoul

*Autumn Showers* is a small version of a painting made in 1889
and which can be seen illustrated opposite page 120 of
*James Caw, William McTaggart: James Maclehose & Sons*, 1917.
Caw identifies how from this time McTaggart's work displays
a 'unified pictorial expression' wherein the human interest and
the landscape are perfectly complementary. McTaggart knew
every lane and byway through the fields around his home and
walking the landscape quickly fed the new subject matter of
rolling countryside. Our picture is dated 1891, so he must have
revisited the subject (as he often did) two years later, but the
same three little girls hunker down by the dirt roadside, one
examining a bird's nest, while the landscape of fields rolls away
and a sky worthy of Constable promises sunshine and showers.

## EA HORNEL (1864–1933)

Opposite: Cat.4, A Woodland Pool, 1900, oil on canvas board, 56 x 22.5 cms. Provenance: The Scottish Gallery, Edinburgh, 1944; Private Collection, London, thence by descent

It is no coincidence that the curators of the magnificent Glasgow Boys exhibition at Kelvingrove Art Gallery in 2010 chose 1900 as their cut-off date. Hornel was to live on until 1933, but his later work became formulaic. In 1900, aged thirty-six, Hornel was at the peak of his powers and still inspired by his eighteen months in Japan from the summer of 1893. Back in Kirkcudbright his subject reprised earlier idyllic rural scenes, essentially like the Japanese examples but with parasols, fans and kimonos now swopped for posies and pinafores.

A Woodland Pool is a pre-eminent example: the tall format, partial subsuming of the figures into the woodland, rich impasto, tonal contrasts and sonorous colour are brilliantly realised without sentimentality.

## ARTHUR MELVILLE
### RSW, ARSA, ARWS, RP, RWS (1855–1904)

Opposite: Cat.5, Hillside, Invertrossachs, 1893,
watercolour, 37 x 54 cms. Provenance: James Strachey
and Alexandra Strachey. Literature: Arthur Melville
by Agnes MacKay, F. Lewis, 1951, p.135

Arthur Melville though he was based in Edinburgh was a close
associate of the Glasgow Boys; going on a trip with James
Guthrie to the Orkneys (1885) and painting with the Boys at
Cockburnspath, where he must have been impressed by the
work of Joseph Crawhall and E.A. Walton and in turn his own
approach would have had an effect on their development.

Although Melville moved to London in 1889, he returned
to Scotland to paint at Brig o' Turk with Joseph Crawhall in
the autumn of 1893. *Hillside, Invertrossachs* is one of around
six watercolours he is known to have painted on this visit
(another being *Autumn, Loch Lomond*, Glasgow Museums
and Art Galleries). This painting is of the south side of
Loch Venacher, between Brig o' Turk and Callander and is a
supreme example of his brilliant watercolour technique and
colour which was to have a profound effect on succeeding
painters, including his godson F.C.B. Cadell.

## DENIS PEPLOE
### RSA (1914 – 1993)

Cat.6, Suilven, c.1959, oil on canvas, 49.5 x 90 cms.
Exhibited: *Denis Peploe, Paintings from the Artist's Studio*,
The Scottish Gallery, Edinburgh, 1984, cat.14

Denis Peploe, the younger son of S.J. Peploe, attended Edinburgh College of Art
and after War service resumed his painting and exhibiting career at The Scottish
Gallery in June 1947. His predominant landscape subject was the West Highlands
and in this powerful work from the late fifties the majestic profile of Suilven,
rising from near sea level dominates the composition.

## WILLIAM GILLIES
### CBE, RSA, RA, PPRSW (1898–1973)

Cat.7, Landscape below Stow, c.1950s, oil on canvas,
63.5 x 76 cms. Exhibited: *Ground Floor Gallery Opening*,
The Scottish Gallery, Edinburgh, 1981; *A Dozen Paintings and
Works on Paper*, The Scottish Gallery, Edinburgh, 2016, ex cat;
*Modern Masters VI*, The Scottish Gallery, Edinburgh, 2017,
cat.32. Provenance: Private collection, Edinburgh

Gillies' subject is the Gala Water beneath Stow with rising
hillside beyond, fields and copses climbing to a high horizon
and a typically dark sky. As with many of Gillies' oils from
the 1950s, his interest is in capturing a certain time and
place, reducing the landscape in front of him to patterns of
flat colour, without making the full leap into abstraction.
This significant oil is one of the finest to come onto the
market in recent years and places Gillies amongst his English
contemporaries at the heart of British modernism.

# JAMES MORRISON
## RSA, RSW (b.1932)

Cat.8, Blue Hills, 15.vii,1998, oil on board, 100 x 150 cms.
Exhibited: *James Morrison, Decades*, The Scottish Gallery, Edinburgh, 2017, cat.5

The genius of a Morrison landscape lies in his absolute adherence to realism, in the sense of truth to what he sees, to the reality of his subject, but without the slavish recording of detail. Legaston is in the heart of Morrison country, just south of the hamlet of Friockheim, the farm and steading seen across the autumn fields, protected by a stand of trees, the air is still and warm, the landscape a perfect illustration for Grassic Gibbon's *Sunset Song*.

## VICTORIA CROWE
### OBE, DHC, FRSE, MA (RCA), RSW, RSW (b.1945)

Cat.9, Large Tree Group, Winter, 2014, etching and screenprint, 50.5 x 71 cm, edition of 250

'Jenny Armstrong was born in 1903 at the farm in the lower Pentland Hills. Victoria Crowe's pictures pay tribute to the life and work of this individual and at the same time record a rural way of life, once common, but now changing so fast that it has evolved beyond recognition.' — John Leighton and James Holloway, *A Shepherd's Life: Paintings of Jenny Armstrong by Victoria Crowe*, Scottish National Portrait Gallery, 2000

Victoria Crowe painted *Large Tree Group* in 1975, and it is an iconic work from the *Shepherd's Life* series. The etching and screenprint made in 2014 pays homage to the impact and continuing memory of Jenny Armstrong. Dovecot Studios, Edinburgh, who celebrated their centenary in 2012, commissioned a large-scale tapestry of *Large Tree Group* which was unveiled in 2013 in the exhibition *Fleece to Fibre: The Making of The Large Tree Group Tapestry* during the Edinburgh International Festival. The tapestry was subsequently acquired for the permanent collection of National Museums Scotland and the painting is now in the collection of Scottish National Gallery of Modern Art.

Cat.10, Victoria Crowe, Twilight, Deeper Shade, 2015, oil on museum board, 68.5 x 99 cms.
Exhibited: *Victoria Crowe, Light on the Landscape*, The Scottish Gallery, Edinburgh, 2016, cat. 14;
*Modern Masters VI*, The Scottish Gallery, Edinburgh, 2017, cat. 46

This painting is from a collection of work that Crowe produced as part of her residency at Dumfries
House in 2015. Her subjects were found whilst walking the grounds at dusk, contemplating the
trees through the moonlight and experiencing the turning season.

## DAVID COOK (b.1957)

Paper Factory at Inverkeithing, 2013, oil on board,
81 x 101.5 cms. Exhibited: *David Cook, Savage Tranquillity*,
The Scottish Gallery, Edinburgh, 2013, cat.47.
Provenance: Purchased from The Scottish Gallery by
Dunfermline District Museum, 2013

'This paper factory was flattened two years back, but used to
stand in Inverkeithing, fascinating me since I was 17 years old.
I would do scribbles on bits of paper as the train hurtled past.
I often think of this spot and attempted to paint it.'
— David Cook, 2014

## GEOFF UGLOW (b.1978)

Cat.11, Union Jack, 2014, oil on board, 51 x 61 cms.
Exhibited: *RSA Open Exhibition*, Royal Scottish Academy,
Edinburgh, 2016; *Modern Masters VI*, The Scottish Gallery,
Edinburgh, 2017, cat. 48

After graduating from Glasgow School of Art in 2000,
Geoff Uglow accepted a studio from Edinburgh City Council
that looked down from the Old City Observatory on Calton
Hill and onto the city. These works from 2014 capture the
same view of Princes Street and the Burns Monument at
different times of day – a spontaneous reaction to the city
in changing light and weather. The raw energy of Uglow's
workmanship is conveyed in the heavy, swirling daubs of paint
that hang off the board as if he has just lifted his brush,
even after the paint has dried.

## PAUL REID (b.1975)

Cat.12, Tree Study (Winter), 2017, oil on canvas, 56 x 45 cms. Exhibited: *Paul Reid, Gods, Heroes and Beasts*, The Scottish Gallery, Edinburgh, 2017, cat.8

Paul Reid's work is informed by his study of the techniques of the Old Masters. With these tools he creates an uncompromising and enthralling world. His hyper-real landscapes are imaginary but take inspiration from locations as varied as the Pentlands and Crete. His landscapes are a vehicle for enigmatic, contemporary narrative, plenished with mythic warriors, philosophers and beasts.

## MATTHEW DRAPER (b.1973)

Top: Cat.13, Sunrise (Part II), Kitchen Window Series No.18, 2016, pastel on paper, 26.5 x 41.5 cms. Exhibited: *Matthew Draper, Amongst the Clouds*, The Scottish Gallery, Edinburgh, 2016, cat.24

Bottom: Cat.14, Impending Storm, The Crags from Blackford, 2016, pastel on paper, 15 x 21 cms. Exhibited: *Matthew Draper, Amongst the Clouds*, The Scottish Gallery, Edinburgh, 2016, cat.31

Matthew Draper identifies himself principally as a draughtsman; drawing being the most unencumbered and immediate form of image-making. His work is made with an intense and energetic immediacy, working instinctively rather than methodically, keeping him physically and emotionally involved in the process. He crushes soft pastels in his hands rubbing the dust into the paper in wide sweeps of colour gradually manipulating the material to build up a layered surface using the ball of his thumb or the heal of his hand.

# THREE

# The Scottish Colourists

F.C.B. Cadell

J.D. Fergusson

George Leslie Hunter

S.J. Peploe

Selection of exhibition catalogues from left to right:
*J.D. Fergusson, La Vie Boheme*, December 2013;
*The Taste of J.W. Blyth*, July 2012;
*The Scottish Colourists in Paris*, May 2003;
*The Scottish Colourists*, August 2016;
*S.J. Peploe, Scotland's First Modernist*, October 2012

Previous: F.C.B. Cadell, Still Life, Tulips, c.1923 (detail)
oil on canvas, 51 x 61 cms. Exhibited: *Festival Exhibition*,
The Royal Scottish Academy, Edinburgh, 1949; Cork Street,
London, The Scottish Gallery, 2012; *Spring Collection*,
The Scottish Gallery, Edinburgh, 2012; *The Scottish Colourists*,
The Scottish Gallery, 2016, cat.6. Provenance: S.J. Peploe
and thence by descent. Sold by The Gallery, 2016. Literature:
Tom Hewlett and Duncan Macmillan, *F.C.B. Cadell*, Lund
Humphries, London, 2011 (p.168)

# The Scottish Colourists

In November 1898 the partners of Aitken Dott & Son bought the painting *A Gypsy Queen* by Samuel John Peploe. Two years before, the partners had formed The Scottish Gallery to identify the picture-dealing part of the firm as distinct from the other businesses – architectural supplies, artist materials, framing, gilding and other services – and determined to represent the best of contemporary Scottish painting.

The picture purchase began a close relationship between the firm (and its senior partner, Peter McOmish Dott) and the artist, then twenty-seven. Dott was a wholehearted adherent of the early paintings and bought three more the next year; a show was arranged for January 1903 that was to be a commercial success and a significant succès d'estime. Peploe went on to become Scotland's first modernist, turning his back on his early success. McOmish Dott was unable to embrace the extraordinary changes in the direction of expressionist colour and the avant-garde that Peploe represented in 1911, but George Proudfoot and subsequent partners continued their support. From the early twenties The Gallery had a joint contract, along with Alex. Reid & Lefevre, to buy work directly from the artist, an arrangement that allowed Peploe to remove himself from the stress of the marketplace and concentrate on work, particularly his new subject of Iona and the magnificent rose and tulip paintings of his maturity. From April 1924, both firms had a similar arrangement with George Leslie Hunter and his only show with The Gallery took place in the autumn. It was a momentous year which saw the exhibition *Les Peintres de l'Écosse Moderne* at the Galerie Barbazanges in Paris, featuring Peploe, Fergusson, Hunter and Cadell. It was also a productive time for Hunter, who worked in Fife, on Loch Lomond and in a Glasgow studio for the most of the next three years. From 1928 he was living mostly in the South of France, based in Saint Paul de Vence, from where he sent back pen and crayon drawings, one fine example of which is in our catalogue.

**In November 1898 the partners of Aitken Dott & Son bought the painting *A Gypsy Queen* by Samuel John Peploe. Two years before, the partners had formed The Scottish Gallery to identify the picture-dealing part of the firm as distinct from the other businesses – architectural supplies, artist materials, framing, gilding and other services – and determined to represent the best of contemporary Scottish painting.**

S.J. Peploe, Still Life with Patterned Cloth and Pink Rose,
c.1918, oil on canvas, 40 x 45 cms. Exhibited: *Modern Masters V*,
The Scottish Gallery, Edinburgh, 2016, cat.33. Provenance:
The late Theodora Hamm Lang of St Paul, Minnesota;
Private Collection, London; Sold by The Gallery, 2016

F.C.B. Cadell showed first with The Gallery in 1909 and
again the following year when his Venetian work was
showcased. The visit, sponsored by his friend Sir Patrick
Ford, had been productive and represented (as with
Peploe and Fergusson in Royan in the same year) his
full engagement with a personal impressionism in which
colour was used for direct expressionist purpose. His
was a precocious early career, brilliant in watercolour,
encouraged by his godfather, Arthur Melville. In oil,
again chiming with the other Colourists, his earlier work
is characterised by rich medium, broad brush marks
and is high in tone, unlike the more sonorous works of
Peploe and Fergusson's early Edinburgh years. His next
show was not until 1932, at a time when picture sales
were in decline and the artist's fortunes at a low ebb,
having moved from his property in Ainslie Place to a
rented flat at 30 Regent Terrace. Cadell had always been
comfortable to be his own agent, using the artist-run
Society of Eight for many of his exhibitions of new work,
and on Iona, where he spent every summer after the
Great War, setting up a daily exhibition of the fruits of
his labour, his manservant Charles Oliver acting as sales
agent, selling to the many wealthy summer visitors, like
David Russell of Markinch and George Service of Cove.

Like Cadell, J.D. Fergusson did not have a consistent
relationship with a commercial gallery. His only lifetime
show with The Scottish Gallery was in 1923 and
significantly included both the small-scale sculpture
he had produced over the preceding few years and
the Highland series of oil paintings, which represent
the artist's engagement with his native landscape and
culture. Twenty years before, he had been one of
the purchasers of work from his friend Peploe's first
exhibition at the gallery, but in the intervening years he
had looked to London and then Paris for his commercial
and spiritual existence. It would only be after his second

flight from the continent, in the face of World War One, that Scotland would take the central place in his work and thoughts. Fergusson was a paragon of the bohemian life and today we can see his work of 1908–1925 as one of the major contributions to British modernism – uncompromising, modernist and brilliant, nothing better than the charcoal drawing *Nude* as seen in this publication (cat.16, p.54).

At no time in the last 120 years would an enquiry after the work of one or all the Colourists have been fruitless at the front desk of The Scottish Gallery. In the decades after their deaths, the firm has represented the estates, included key works in survey exhibitions, sold works into national museums and galleries and fostered and expended the reputations of the artists, stressing their significance in a British and European context. This year sees the launch of the Scottish Colourist Foundation, whose aims are to continue to enhance the national and international reputations of these four painters through exhibitions, publications and advocacy, driven by the passion and knowledge of our director Guy Peploe.

*S.J. Peploe* by Guy Peploe, Lund Humphries, 2012

# F.C.B. CADELL
## RSA (1883–1937)

Opposite: *Interior, 6 Ainslie Place*, c.1921, oil on canvas, 76 x 56 cms.
Exhibited: *The Scottish Colourists in Paris*, The Scottish Gallery,
Galerie Francis Barlier. Paris, 2003. Provenance: Miss M Rough,
Edinburgh; John Magee Ltd, Belfast; Aitken Dott & Son, The Scottish
Gallery; Major David Russell, Fife; Sold by The Gallery, 2003

Cadell was twelve years younger than S.J. Peploe but was greatly
precocious and was producing very capable watercolours and
drawings in his early teens. Half French, he was taken to France and
Munich by his mother for artistic education and some very fine, freely
painted farmyard paintings date from this early period. Despite his
sophistication, Cadell's most natural habitat was the west Highlands,
Iona in particular, and he made only a few painting trips to France after
the war. He produced some of his most brilliant colourist works while
staying with the Peploes in Cassis in 1924. Very fashion-conscious, his
work before 1914 had an Edwardian opulence and breadth unique in
Scottish painting. By the twenties his work had a hard edge with clear
colour, chiming with the Jazz Age; the compositions
have a deco stylishness full of sophistication of
concept and originality of palette. He is as original
and distinctive a voice as any in Scottish painting.

Right: *Jack and Tommy Book*, 1916, hard cover,
32 x 25.5 cms, published by Grant Richards, London

*Jack & Tommy* was published to benefit the War
effort. Cadell himself enlisted as a private soldier
in the Argylls, was twice wounded and eventually
accepted a commission, finishing the War looking after
prisoners of war. On leave, dining in London with his
kinsman and friend the Duke of Argyll he caused some
confusion amongst other officer diners at the Savoy
in his Savile Row tailored private's uniform.

49

Cat.15, F.C.B. Cadell, Traigh Geal, Erraid, Argyll, c.1925, oil on panel, 36.5 x 45 cms. Exhibited: *The Scottish Colourists*, The Scottish Gallery, Edinburgh, 2016, cat.9. Provenance: Major David Russell, Rothes, Fife, thence by descent

Erraid is a tidal island off the tip of the Ross off Mull, a mile or so south of Iona. She is known to Robert Louis Stevenson readers as the location of the shipwrecked Davie Balfour, stuck there for four days in the rain eating limpets before realising he could walk off at low tide. Stevenson had come with his father aged 20 when the family engineering firm was engaged to build a lighthouse on the outer torran rocks (the very place Balfour's ship was lost) and the quarry workers' cottages are still occupied today. This is the only known work of this subject, the view taken towards Jura from the island across the tidal narrows. It is as fresh and brilliant as any of his Argyll works, perhaps inspired by the very wildness and natural beauty of the place and a relief from 'the usual horrors of Ben More, the Burg, and Loch Na Keal'.

# J.D. FERGUSSON
## RBA (1874–1961)

Born in Leith, J.D. Fergusson studied at the Trustees Academy in Edinburgh before travelling to Paris, where he was one of the first British artists to engage with French modernist painting, alongside S.J. Peploe. Fergusson spent most of his professional life in France and even in the last fifteen years of his life, when his base was in Glasgow, summers were spent with Margaret Morris's summer school at Cap d'Antibes. Bohemian Paris was the ideal milieu for Fergusson and he had a huge circle of friends of many nationalities. He became a sociétaire of the Salon d'Automne and an exhibitor at the Salon des Indépendants. He had a major exhibition at the Doré Gallery in New Bond Street in London in 1914, where he was forced to return from Antibes at the outbreak of war. After the successful show in Paris in 1924 he took a studio at the Hôtel des Académies and divided his life between Paris and London until he and Meg moved to Glasgow in 1939. In 1931 he exhibited at *Les Peintres Écossais* exhibition at the Galerie Georges Petit in Paris, where his work *La Déesse de la Rivière* was purchased by the French government. In 1954 he was honoured with a travelling retrospective exhibition organised by the Arts Council of Great Britain.

Fergusson in his Paris studio, c.1910
© The Fergusson Gallery, Perth & Kinross Council

The Conversation, c.1907, oil on panel, 26.5 x 33.5 cms.
Exhibited: *Exhibition of 20th Century British Paintings*,
National Gallery, London, 1940, cat. 358; *Modern Masters V*,
The Scottish Gallery, Edinburgh, 2016, cat.16.
Provenance: Collection of J.W. Blyth, Kirkcaldy;
Private Collection, London. Sold by The Gallery, 2016

This small panel was sold by the Gallery in 2016. It belongs
at the end of the artist's early period in France, along with
such images as *Fireworks Dieppe* and the cafe sketches, later
published in a book by the artist's widow. As an immaculately
dressed bohemian Fergusson was able to move between the
beau and demi mondes, and indeed Paris in these early years
of the 20th Century was if not a classless society one in which
the classes continuously intermingled. The beautifully turned
out women in hats and long dresses, so beloved by Fergusson's
conté crayon, were more often milliners' assistants on their
lunch breaks than grand dames.

J.D. Fergusson and S.J. Peploe at Paris-Plage, c.1907

From the early 1900s Fergusson spent many summers
exploring the coast of north-west France often accompanied
by S.J. Peploe. Both artists were particularly taken by the
resort of Paris-Plage. It was at this time that both artists were
at the height of their engagement with Impressionism.

Cat.16, J.D. Fergusson, Nude, Paris, 1912, charcoal and chalk, 36 x 23.7 cms.
Provenance: Anne Estelle Rice; O Raymond Drey, Manchester; David Drey Esq,
Withington House, Manchester

Fergusson was a prolific draftsman, seldom without a sketchbook. In the earliest
period, his drawings with conte or pencil are delicate and depict domestic or street
observations. In the studio he tended to work directly in oil and it is only when he
was established in his first Paris studio from 1907 that the nude model became a
regular subject. He worked quickly, changing the pose but rarely using any pentimenti,
such was the confidence of his line. In the earlier Paris years he also made a prodigious
quantity of on-the-spot café drawings, some quite 'worked up', and a selection was
published in 1974 in a volume entitled *Café Drawings in Edwardian Paris* as a centenary
tribute to Fergus, with an introduction by Margaret Morris.

By 1907 he had met and become involved with Anne Estelle Rice. She had come
from Philadelphia to work as a fashion illustrator, but Fergusson persuaded her to
become a painter. They were together until the autumn of 1913, when the relationship
ended and she married the critic O. Raymond Drey and Fergusson began his lifelong
relationship with Morris. From the summer of 1911, the art journal *Rhythm* was
published, with Fergusson as art editor, a position he maintained for a year, and Drey
as one of the many young English literary contributors. The illustrations were selected
for graphic strength, with artwork by Fergusson, Rice, Peploe, Picasso, Derain,
Othon Friesz and many others in black and white.

*Nude, Paris* is an outstanding drawing from this period. It is unusually large, drawn on
a coloured sheet and is in charcoal and pastel. The subject is undoubtedly Rice and was
a gift to her, which accounts for the provenance by descent from her husband and son.

Cat.17, J.D. Fergusson, Street, Pourville, 1926, pencil and
watercolour, 33 x 27 cms. Exhibited: *Modern Masters VI*,
The Scottish Gallery, Edinburgh, cat.5.
Provenance: Private collection

Pourville is a beach resort flanked by cliffs just south of Dieppe.
As 'Green Beach' it was one of the objectives in the Dieppe
Raid of 1942 and saw heavy allied casualties. In 1926 it would
have been a quiet village and a likely stopover for Fergusson
and Meg as they travelled from London to the South of France,
perhaps scouting for an alternative venue for a Margaret Morris
dance retreat. In Meg's biography on Fergusson she describes
Pourville as 'a charming little town, still unspoiled, with good
bathing and charming country around'. Fergusson's vigorous
wash drawings display a typical strong, modern structure while
being true to place.

Cat.18, J.D. Fergusson, Hills, Pourville, c.1926, watercolour,
33 x 27 cms. Exhibited: *Annual Exhibition*,
St Andrews Fine Art, St Andrews, 1989, cat. 62;
*Modern Masters VI*, The Scottish Gallery, Edinburgh, cat.5.
Provenance: Private collection, Edinburgh

Opposite: Cat.19, J.D. Fergusson, Margaret and Willy Peploe at Hotel Panorama, Cassis, 1931, oil on canvas, 61 x 56.5 cms. Exhibited: Cork Street, London, The Scottish Gallery, 2011; *Spring Collection*, The Scottish Gallery, Edinburgh, April 2012; *J.D. Fergusson*, Portland Gallery, London, November 2013, cat. 15; *J.D. Fergusson, La Vie Boheme*, The Scottish Gallery, Edinburgh, December 2013, cat. 73; The Scottish Colourists, The Scottish Gallery, 2016, cat. 16. Provenance: Gifted to S.J. Peploe, thence by descent; Fragmentary label verso 'Mrs. Peploe and Bill at Cassis, Hotel du Panorama'; labels also for artist's addresses in Paris and Glasgow; label stating picture belongs to Willy Peploe, April 1944.

In August 1913, Fergusson was in Cassis with his partner, Anne Estelle Rice, accompanying S.J. Peploe, his wife, Margaret, and their son, Willy. It was both artists' first visit to the South of France and their choice of the small fishing village near Marseilles may have been inspired by the many French painters who had worked there before, including Paul Signac. It was Fergusson who recalled persuading Peploe to accompany him, after seeing a poster with the name 'Cassis' on it near his Paris studio. Fergusson wrote in 1945 in his *Memories of Peploe* that at first he thought it would be too hot for 'Bill', but 'he decided to take the risk. We arrived to find it quite cool and Bill didn't suffer at all. We had his (third) birthday there and after a lot of consideration chose a bottle of Château Lafite instead of champagne. Lafite now always means to me that happy lunch on the verandah overlooking Cassis Bay, sparkling in the sunshine.' As in Royan three years before, both painters worked chiefly on panel, although Fergusson used several canvasses and both made many sketches, particularly of the harbour and its traffic of schooners.

It may have been a difficult time for Fergusson and Rice, who were to separate soon thereafter; Fergusson had already met Margaret Morris in the spring, when she had brought a troupe of her dancers to Paris to perform at the Marigny Theatre. Fergusson, whose Paris studio had been demolished, decided to stay in the south. By Christmas, he was renting a little house at Cap d'Antibes, where he persuaded Morris to join him and where they spent the summer of the next year before the outbreak of war forced their return to London.

The group stayed in the Hotel Panorama, which forms the backdrop to the portrait, with its distinctive round pediment on the façade and screened verandah below. Peploe painted the same view when he returned with Willy, Denis and Margaret in 1924.

At this time, Fergusson was seeking more structure in his compositions; the simplification of motif recalls later Cézanne. The paint was applied in short, directional brush marks and the palette restrained. In recollection, he has captured the calm strength of his subject with her young child, confident in motherhood.

J.D. Fergusson, Margaret and Willy Peploe, Cassis, c.1913

## GEORGE LESLIE HUNTER (1877–1931)

Born in Rothesay in 1879, George Leslie Hunter emigrated
to California in 1892, where his father bought a farm.
He spent all his time drawing and when his family came
back in 1900 he stayed to become part of the bohemian
lifestyle of San Francisco. He earned money through
illustration work for newspapers and magazines. He
went to New York with friends and then on to Paris in
1904, working in each city for a few months. Back in San
Francisco he lost everything in the 1906 earthquake and
shortly thereafter returned permanently to Scotland.
He had his first solo exhibition with Alexander Reid in
Glasgow in 1915, an association that continued until his
death in 1931. From 1923 he exhibited with Peploe and
Cadell as the Three Scottish Colourists and he spent
much of the twenties in France, often subsidised by
Reid and a coterie of dedicated collectors including
T.J. Honeyman, who wrote his biography after his
untimely death at fifty-four.

**Opposite: Robinson Crusoe's House, Lower Largo, c.1922,
oil on panel, 35 x 25.5 cms. Provenance: Private Collection,
Edinburgh; Sold by The Gallery, 2013**

Fife proved one of Hunter's most productive painting grounds
in the early twenties. He painted and drew the villages and
harbours of the East Neuk as well the interior of the ancient
Kingdom; the mills, farms and cottages with their distinctive red
pantile roofs provided inspiration. He depicted the village street
at Lower Largo several times, curving to its conclusion at the
beach and the cottage known as Robinson Crusoe's House; the
village was home of the sailor Alexander Selkirk whose four years
on a desert island inspired Daniel Defoe's 1719 tale. The cottage
sits atop the sea wall and Hunter must have sat on the beach.
As with the best of his work, it is made with quick, decisive
drawing with the brush and lyrical colour.

Cat.20, George Leslie Hunter, Juan-les-Pins, c.1928, ink and crayon,
30 x 37 cms. Provenance: Alexander Reid & Lefevre, London

Hunter spent much of the late twenties in the South of France,
sometimes based at Saint Paul de Vence, but also visiting Antibes,
Cassis, Villefranche and Juan-les-Pins. While his dealer, Dr T.J.
Honeyman, then a partner in the firm of Reid & Lefevre, waited for
news of painting success to fulfil a longstanding commitment to a
one-man show, his output was in large restricted to pen and crayon
drawings, like our example. It was a practical medium in which he
could work quickly in front of the subject, here capturing a carriage
passing by a lush palm tree on a bright, fresh Mediterranean day.

## SAMUEL JOHN PEPLOE
### RSA (1871–1935)

Born in 1871, S.J. Peploe is the senior
of the four Scottish Colourists.
Peploe had his first exhibition at
The Scottish Gallery in 1903 and a
lifelong association with us until his
untimely death in 1935. He lived in
Paris from 1910 until 1912, where
his work changed radically, from
paintings reminiscent of Manet and
Sargent to brilliant Fauvist works
that placed him in the vanguard of
British modernism. By the time
of his death aged sixty-four in
1935, he was recognised as a great
painter, but only by a small coterie
of collectors and curators, like Ion
Harrison, T.J. Honeyman, Jack Blyth
and Stanley Cursiter. His reputation
today is secure and growing in some
part thanks to the strength of the
marketplace where The Scottish
Gallery has been a consistent
advocate under the leadership of
Guy Peploe whose biography was
first published in 2000.

S.J. Peploe in his studio at Devon Place, Edinburgh,
c.1902–1904. Note the glass vase with similar flower
arrangement as Still Life with Roses (Cat.21) sits
on the mantelpiece.

Opposite: Page from S.J. Peploe exhibition catalogue,
C.W. Kraushaar Galleries, New York, 1928

## S. J. Peploe—Autobiography

Born Edinburgh, 1871, son of a banker, educated there, Edinburgh Collegiate School and University. Thought in turns of being a soldier, minister, indigo planter, lawyer, farmer, and other pursuits, but preferred doing nothing as long as possible ; the ideal life is the lounger.

At the age of twenty (though not really tired of doing nothing) reading Carlyle and Ruskin was " awakened " to Art (a nice easy life, out-of-doors life). Got enthusiastic and worked hard ; went to Paris—Julien's under Bouguereau (damned old fool), then afterwards in Life School in Edinburgh. Took studio in Edinburgh, produced some masterpieces and a lot of failures. Continued like this till 1910 when married ; had to work hard. Family appeared—had to work harder still. At that time Paris (1911), a very lively time. Came home again, more family appeared—had to work really hard. This has gone on till present time.

There is no end to Art.

Cat.21, S.J. Peploe, Still Life with Roses, c.1898, oil on panel, 35 x 26.5 cms. Provenance: Willy Peploe, thence by descent

*Still Life with Roses* displays the simplicity and sophistication of Peploe's still lifes. His props are confined to cloth, fan and vase with two rose heads, the space created with a series of subtle triangulations. A fallen rose petal (while not necessarily laden with symbolic significance) is completely necessary for the balance of the composition. Peploe began to exhibit about this time and, never prolific, this work might well have been included in his first solo show at The Scottish Gallery in 1903.

S.J. Peploe, The Lobster, c. 1901, oil on canvas, 41 x 51 cms.
Exhibited: Aitken Dott & Son, The Scottish Gallery, 1903;
Loan Exhibition, Kirkcaldy Museum and Art Gallery, 1928; *S.J.
Peploe Memorial Exhibition*, Aitken Dott & Son, The Scottish
Gallery, Edinburgh, 1936, cat.39; *S.J. Peploe Memorial Exhibition*,
McLellan Galleries, Glasgow, 1937, cat.64; *Empire Exhibition*,
Scotland, 1938; *Exhibition of Scottish Art*, Royal Academy of
Arts, London, 1939; *S.J. Peploe*, National Gallery of Scotland,
1941, cat.6; British Council and Fine Arts Department
Exhibition, Cairo & Algiers, 1944; *The Scottish Colourists*, Ewan
Mundy Fine Art, Glasgow, 1989, cat.1; *S.J. Peploe, Paintings and
Drawings*, Duncan Miller Fine Art, London, 1993, cat.2; *The
Scottish Colourists*, Royal Academy of Arts, 2000, cat.59; *The
Taste of J.W. Blyth*, The Scottish Gallery, 2012. Provenance:
J.J. Cowan; William Home Cook; J.W. Blyth, Kirkcaldy and
by descent. Sold by The Gallery, 2012. Illustrated: Stanley
Cursiter, *Peploe*, Thomas Nelson and Sons Ltd, 1947, Plate 5;
Guy Peploe, *S.J. Peploe*, Lund Humphries, 2012, Plate 50

By the time of the Peploe's death in 1935, James Caw had
come to recognise him as one of Scotland's greatest painters.
Caw was the biographer of his father-in-law, William McTaggart,
and wrote Scottish Painting: Past and Present, published in 1908.
He was the director of the Scottish National Gallery and the
Scottish National Portrait Gallery from 1907–1930. When he
reviewed Peploe's first exhibition in 1903, his praise was heavily
qualified; he identified a 'perverse taste for the ugly or the
bizarre in figure and landscape' and a lack of subtlety of vision.
Certainly Peploe's early work is bold and his subjects not chosen
for their inherent beauty; even The Lobster (which Caw singles
out for particular praise) is a difficult subject; an admirable lunch
and a complex, fascinating creature, but certainly a challenge to
the painter. Peploe has made out of it one of his masterpieces.
This painting was sold by The Gallery in 2012 in the seminal
exhibition *The Taste of J.W. Blyth*.

"In his painting he tried to find the essentials by persistent trial. He worked all the time from nature but never imitated it. He often took a long time to make contact with a place and was discouraged by failure. He wanted to be sure before he started and seemed to believe that you could be sure. I don't think he wanted to have a struggle on the canvas: he wanted to be sure of a thing and do it. That gave his picture something."

J.D. Fergusson, Memories of Peploe
(Scottish Art Review, 1962)

S.J. Peploe, White Roses and Fruit, c.1921, oil on canvas, 51 x 40.5 cms.
Exhibited: *Three Scottish Colourists*, Fine Art Society, Edinburgh and London, 1977, cat. 40; *S.J. Peploe*, The Scottish Gallery, Edinburgh, 2012, cat.23.
Provenance: Private Collection, London; Sold by The Gallery, 2012.
Illustrated: *S.J. Peploe*, Guy Peploe, Lund Humphries, 2012, Plate 137

Cat.22, S.J. Peploe, White Sands, Iona, oil on panel, 37.5 x 44 cms. Exhibited: *Memorial Exhibition of Paintings by S.J. Peploe*, as 'Rough Sea, Iona', The McLellan Galleries, Glasgow, February 1937; *Pictures from a Private Collection*, The Thistle Foundation, The McLellan Galleries, Glasgow, March 1951, cat. 44; *Two Scottish Colourists, Samuel John Peploe and F.C.B. Cadell*, The Lefevre Gallery, London, November and December 1988, cat. 7; *F.C.B. Cadell and S.J. Peploe – Paintings of Iona*, The Scottish Gallery, Edinburgh, September 2014. Provenance: Alexander Reid, Glasgow; Aitken Dott & Son, The Scottish Gallery, Edinburgh; Major Ion Harrison

This work comes from the Harrison collection and has been widely exhibited and praised. Peploe's subject is the view from the north beach to Gribun head on the Burg with waves breaking on the western end of Eilean Annraidh (the island of storms). The day is one that Peploe preferred; he wrote to his friend William Macdonald in November 1923: We had miserable weather in Iona this year – worst in living memory – gales and rain the whole time. I got very little done. But that kind of weather suits Iona: the rocks and distant shores seen through falling rain, veil behind veil, take on an elusive quality, and when the light shines through one has visions of rare beauty. I think I prefer it these days to your blue skies and clear distances.

/ FOUR /

# The Painting Schools
of Scotland

# The Painting Schools of Scotland

Many cultural commentators have attempted to make generalisations about Scottish painting: something in the water, or even the whisky, a Celtic commonality or a Presbyterian work ethic. These musings are seldom worthwhile and, in any case, do not begin to explain the wealth and diversity of the history of Scottish art. In the last hundred years or so we have the four Scottish art colleges to thank. The Edinburgh School might contain artists as diverse as William Gillies and David Michie, but the description is more meaningful than the list of alumni of Edinburgh College of Art since its inception in 1909. The Scottish Gallery provided the nearest and most significant opportunity for various members of the Edinburgh School to exhibit, at first in mixed exhibitions. MacTaggart was the earliest to have a solo exhibition in 1929, followed in the 1940s by shows for Gillies, Adam Bruce Thomson, Anne Redpath, Robin Philipson and others. A second wave of Edinburgh graduates (many of them influenced by the previous generation) began exhibiting in the late 1950s and early 1960s, principally David McClure, John Houston, Elizabeth Blackadder and David Michie.

The Glasgow School of Art, world renowned because of Charles Rennie Mackintosh's magnificent building has given us William Crosbie, Robert Colquhoun and Robert MacBryde and then David Donaldson, Joan Eardley, Duncan Shanks, Jimmy Robertson, George Devlin, Archie Forrest and Alison Watt the latter group all adherents of the Donaldson approach of direct, gestural painting and colour construction.

In Dundee, at the Duncan of Jordanstone College of Art and Design, the arrival of Alberto Morrocco from Aberdeen in 1950 and his recruitment of David McClure and then the Glasgow graduates Jack Knox and James Morrison, as well as the determined, conservative influence of James McIntosh Patrick, created a lively, progressive atmosphere which eventually fostered the careers of many successful painters including Philip Braham, Derrick Guild, Robert Macmillan and Paul Reid. At Gray's School of Art in Aberdeen, Ian Fleming also

> Many cultural commentators have attempted to make generalisations about Scottish painting; something in the water, or even the whisky, a celtic commonality or a Presbyterian work ethic. These musings are seldom worthwhile and in any case, do not begin to explain the wealth and diversity of the history of Scottish art.

Previous: Glasgow School of Art, GSA Archives and Collections

Right and overleaf: Edinburgh College of Art, School of Drawing, Painting, Design and Sculpture, 1949–50

EDWARD GAGE

HARRY MORE GORDON

W.J.L. BAILLIE

Alastair Flattely

2ⁿᵈ ROW
AMUSA REID
DAVID McCLURE

FRANCES WALKER

CHARLES
PULSFORD

ROBIN
PHILIPSON

DEREK
CLARKE

JOHN HUNTER

NORMAN
FORREST

ANN
HENDERSON

AN

EDINBURGH CO

SCHOOL OF DRAWING, PAINTING,

JOHN HOUSTON    DAVID MICHIE     RICHARD DEMARCO

3rd ROW ADAM ROBSON    2nd ROW RODICK CARMICHAEL

ERIC SCHILSKY    W. G. GILLIES    ELDER DICKSON    PENELOPE BEATON    R. HENDERSON BLYTH    1st ROW SEATED DAPHNE DYCE SHARP FOUNDER 57 GALLERY    3rd ROW BARBARA BALMER    2nd ROW ALASTAIR PARK

ADAM BRUCE THOMSON

EGE OF ART.

ESIGN & SCULPTURE.    1949 - 50.

E. R. YERBURY & SON
90 & 92 MOR.INGSIDE ROAD
EDINBURGH, 10

built up a talented teaching department, including Robert Henderson Blyth. His insistence on the importance of drawing was carried forward by Alexander Fraser, nurturing the talents of Barry McGlashan, Joe Fan and others whose work forms an identifiable whimsical realism associated with the art school. These broad identifiers deriving from the four colleges are useful streams, but by no means the whole picture. It is necessary for the student to rebel and go against the tutor, for the young artist to seek brotherhood outside the institutions of the colleges, RSA or RGI. The Society of Eight, the Edinburgh Group, New Scottish Group and Glasgow Group were all collectives seeking to find opportunities outside the mainstream. From 1984, the New Glasgow Boys, like their progenitors from the 1880s, exhibited together and were marketed together with little interest in gaining membership of the academies. With time and maturity those who managed not to burn out would become the next generation of tutors and Academicians. Outwith the four well known colleges the prestigious Patrick Allan Fraser School at Hospitalfield in Arbroath, the nurturing atmosphere of the Leith School of Art and many excellent art courses available at technical and further education colleges have added greatly to Scotland's artistic culture.

Many Scottish artist graduates escaped their colleges and country by making their career in England or further afield, like Eduardo Paolozzi, William Gear and Alan Davie, three towering figures whose reputations have never been framed in a Scottish context. Many more also sought port-graduate placements in London at the Royal Academy Schools, Royal College, Slade, Camberwell and Central Schools, the latter strongly associated with the Scots William Johnstone and Dawyck Haig. Thousands of others will have carried their formative experiences into schools, studios or alternative careers around the globe. While The Scottish Gallery has no restriction on the artists it can represent in its programme the wealth of talent that has emerged from further art education and the close relationship between The Gallery and the colleges has been of vital importance.

ROBERT HENDERSON BLYTH
RSA, RSW (1919–1970)

Bobby Blyth, as he was known amongst his fellow artists, was a popular, familiar figure in the academic and institutional corridors, in Edinburgh and Aberdeen. He took his diploma at Glasgow School of Art before serving in the Army Medical Corps from 1941 until VE Day. Gillies then offered him work at Edinburgh before he moved to Aberdeen in 1954. He had already become a friend of the young students Houston and Blackadder, with whom he remained close. His response to War had been in a few surrealist influenced subject pictures but his subsequent development was in lyrical landscape owing something to Gillies and English neo-romanticism.

Cat.23, Kinnoul Hill, watercolour, 40 x 53 cms.
Exhibited: *Modern Masters V*, The Scottish Gallery, Edinburgh, 2016, cat.1

Gillies and Blyth often worked together in the Highlands or east coast of Scotland, and at times their work became very similar, both favouring a pen and wash technique. This scene is looking west to the summit of Kinnoull Hill near Perth, Kinnoull Tower perched on top of the cliff face. The artist uses vivid, non-naturalistic colours, lime and bottle-greens resonating with each other to enliven the subject. Later, in both oil and watercolour, Blyth used less drawing, favouring a colour-field, near abstract approach.

## WILLIAM GILLIES
### CBE, RSA, RA, PPRSW (1898–1973)

William Gillies was a painter's painter. His high horizons, darkening skies, unusual viewpoints – seeing a subject where most would drive by – and the solid confidence in the worth of a life dedicated to art was quiet inspiration to generations of artists he guided through their diplomas at the Edinburgh College of Art. Many would be brought back to become tutors on his staff where an unswerving loyalty created an atmosphere of possibility and productivity. His commitment to the Scottish landscape, his productivity (there was no time for doubt and hesitation in front of the subject) manifested in an enormously productive relationship with The Scottish Gallery in the post War decades and today one of the certainties is that we shall always represent his work in our stock and exhibition plans.

Opposite: Cat.24, Kippford, c.1949, ink drawing, 43 x 55.9 cms. Provenance: Dr Robert A. Lillie Collection, cat. 593; British Linen Bank, Edinburgh

Gillies made several pen studies of sailing boats at Kippford on the Solway and at least one oil painting. As ever his spare, informative drawing renders a full understanding of the subject, here drawn at low tide with a view across the water to the village and hill beyond.

Left: William Gillies at Loch Tummel, 1936. Courtesy of Royal Scottish Academy Archives (Gillies Bequest)

## DENIS PEPLOE
### RSA (1914–1993)

Opposite: Cat.25, Ben Damh, oil on canvas, 63.5 x 76 cms.
Exhibited: *Denis Peploe, Paintings from the Artist's Studio*,
The Scottish Gallery, Edinburgh, 1984, no.23

Having taken his diploma at Edinburgh College of Art and
then spent several years on post-dip travel, to France, Italy,
Yugoslavia and in particular Spain, Peploe had six years of War
service with little chance to pick up a paint brush. He would
go on to teach at Edinburgh working on still life and figure
paintings from a studio at home and resuming a successful
exhibiting career at The Scottish Gallery in 1985.

Immediately after the war, when he had ended up in the
Special Operations Executive in North Africa and then Italy,
Denis Peploe threw himself into work and in particular the
mountain landscape of the West Highlands. Often based in
Plockton, where his friends Torquil and Isobel Nicolson had
moved to the Old Manse, he would drive, walk and sail to
remote places and capture the rugged terrain, experience
and record the volatile weather and find an equivalent in his
impasto and palette for the ancient rocks of Torridon
and Assynt.

This view is of Ben Damh over Loch an Eoin, and Peploe has
most likely walked in from north of Loch Carron with his
materials, perhaps starting from Coulags, a ten-mile round
trip over rough ground.

Left: Denis Peploe. Photo: Wilhelmina Barns-Graham,
courtesy of the Wilhelmina Barns-Graham Trust

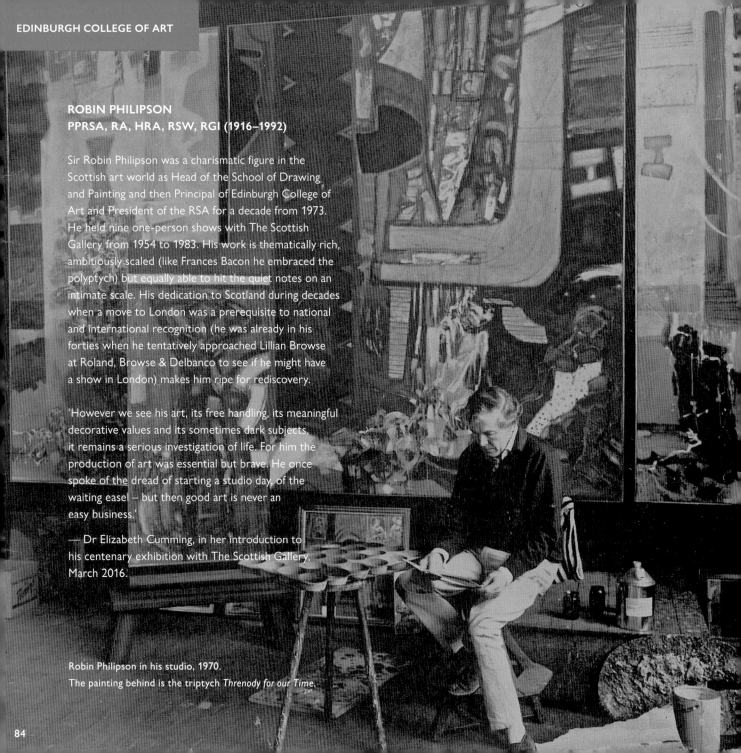

## ROBIN PHILIPSON
### PPRSA, RA, HRA, RSW, RGI (1916–1992)

Sir Robin Philipson was a charismatic figure in the
Scottish art world as Head of the School of Drawing
and Painting and then Principal of Edinburgh College of
Art and President of the RSA for a decade from 1973.
He held nine one-person shows with The Scottish
Gallery from 1954 to 1983. His work is thematically rich,
ambitiously scaled (like Frances Bacon he embraced the
polyptych) but equally able to hit the quiet notes on an
intimate scale. His dedication to Scotland during decades
when a move to London was a prerequisite to national
and international recognition (he was already in his
forties when he tentatively approached Lillian Browse
at Roland, Browse & Delbanco to see if he might have
a show in London) makes him ripe for rediscovery.

'However we see his art, its free handling, its meaningful
decorative values and its sometimes dark subjects,
it remains a serious investigation of life. For him the
production of art was essential but brave. He once
spoke of the dread of starting a studio day, of the
waiting easel – but then good art is never an
easy business.'

— Dr Elizabeth Cumming, in her introduction to
his centenary exhibition with The Scottish Gallery,
March 2016.

Robin Philipson in his studio, 1970.
The painting behind is the triptych *Threnody for our Time*.

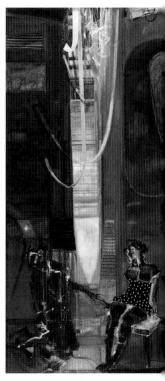

Cat.26, Threnody for our Time, 1971 (Triptych), oil and vinyl toluene on canvas,
left: 274 x 142 cms, middle: 274 x 228.5 cms, right: 274 x 142 cms.
Exhibited: *Robin Philipson Retrospective*, Edinburgh College of Art, Edinburgh, 1989, cat. 71;
*Sir Robin Philipson Retrospective Exhibition*, The Scottish Gallery, Edinburgh, 2006, cat. 1;
*Robin Philipson – 100, Centenary Exhibition*, The Scottish Gallery, Edinburgh, March 2016, cat. 17.
Provenance: The Artist's Estate

Philipson possessed the élan of the Renaissance master in his concept. The broad gesture, mastery
of space, balance of detail and structure are all worthy of Titian. In *Threnody for our Time* there is a
Venetian warmth of colour and exoticism which recalls the sixteenth century master. But it is to
a twentieth century master that the most meaningful comparisons can be made; to Francis Bacon.
The triptych format, the claustrophobic psychological space, distorted or tortured human presence
and triumphant arm-wrestle with the materials are closely present in this work and Bacon's
*Three Studies for Figures at the Base of a Crucifixion*, 1962 (Guggenheim Museum, New York).

## DAVID MICHIE
### OBE, RSA, PSSA, FRSA, RGI, FECA
### (1928–2015)

Born in San Raphael, France and the son of painter Anne Redpath, David Michie graduated from ECA in 1953 following a travelling scholarship to Italy with fellow student John Houston. He lectured at Gray's in Aberdeen and from 1961–1982 at ECA from where he retired in 1990 as Head of School of Drawing and Painting. He died in Edinburgh in 2015, and The Scottish Gallery held his Memorial Exhibition in March 2017. Public collections include HM The Queen, National Galleries of Scotland, Glasgow Museums and Aberdeen Art Galleries and Museums.

'If I hadn't been a painter, I've not the slightest idea what I would have done, but I'm pleased I spent my life painting. For better or for worse, I've inflicted my paintings on the world but I paint because I've had such endless entertainment from what I've found around me…'

— David Michie speaking to filmmaker Sana Bilgrami, 24th June 2015

David Michie in his studio, 1995.
Photo: Eric Thorburn

Cat.27, Lilypads and Lupins, oil on canvas, 100 x 100 cms. Exhibited: *David Michie – Memorial Exhibition*, The Scottish Gallery, Edinburgh, March 2017, ex.cat. Provenance: Private collection, Bathgate

In *Lilypads and Lupins* David Michie is able to coral into his composition a cornucopia of natural phenomena. Michie is less interested in the still life form but prefers instead to take a seemingly random slice of real life and with a conductors skill he marshals nature's unruliness into a wholly satisfying composition, which still crackles with life and colour.

## JOHN HOUSTON
### OBE, RSA, RSW, RGI (1930–2008)

John Houston, who gained his diploma in 1952 and completed his travelling scholarship with David Michie in 1954, is regarded alongside his wife Elizabeth Blackadder, as the key figure in the continuation of The Edinburgh School. His senior position at the College and profile in art education, for which he received an OBE in 1990 did not prevent him from travelling extensively, including to Japan, and having a prodigious exhibiting career, showing twelve times with The Scottish Gallery over fifty years.

Houston pushed his response to the natural phenomena of sunset and rise, which had always inspired him, to a dramatic, expressionist resolution in works like *Lake at Sunset*. His admiration for the northern European romanticism of Emil Nolde and the expressionism of Ernst Ludwig Kirchner is given full rein, but in a language of confidence that is his own achievement. Houston had twelve one-person shows with The Scottish Gallery from 1960. For his final exhibition in 2007, Guy Peploe wrote the foreword:

'Houston's paintings have as many moods as landscape under an ever-changing sky; from the ecstatic to the sombre, from vivid sunset to the gloom of the night sky over the sea. His emotional response to his subject is tempered by his painter's experience; sometimes a thin watercolour wash enlivened with flecks of pastel will be perfectly sufficient, in the best oriental tradition, to capture soft summer light over still water. At other times he deploys an impasto as thick as Frank Auerbach to represent the weight of a cornfield after heavy rain. All responses are true to his experience, to the place and to the day, made permanent in oil, watercolour and pastel.'

Opposite: Cat.28, Lake at Sunset, 1989–90, oil on canvas, 100 x 100 cms.
Exhibited: *John Houston, Festival Exhibition*, The Scottish Gallery, Edinburgh, August 1990, cat. 71; *Modern Masters II*, The Scottish Gallery, 2014, cat. 17

John Houston drawing
at the Bass Rock.
Photo: Elizabeth Blackadder

## ELIZABETH BLACKADDER
### DBE, RA, RSA, RSW, RGI (b.1931)

Many of Scotland's most talented art students have benefitted from the award of bursaries and travelling scholarships. Andrew Grant (1830–1924) an Edinburgh merchant and Liberal politician endowed a gallery in The College and a scholarship in his name which has benefited many dozens of students, particularly through the austerity of the post-War decades including Houston, Blackadder and David Michie. The other colleges have many of their own schemes and access to post-graduate funding from the AHRC (Arts and Humanities Research Council) and without the support of The School of Art William Crosbie would not have been able to study with Leger in Paris, or The Roberts and later John Byrne make their Italian journeys.

John Houston & Elizabeth Blackadder, Salonika, 1954

Cat.29, Fife Farm near Burntisland, c.1952, ink on paper, 33 x 45 cms.
Exhibited: *Elizabeth Blackadder – Decades*, The Scottish Gallery, Edinburgh, 2016, ex.cat;
*Modern Masters VI*, The Scottish Gallery, Edinburgh, 2017, cat.10. Provenance: Private collection

This early sketchbook drawing dates from the artist's time at Edinburgh College of Art. The high
horizon may take influence from her tutor and friend William Gillies, but the nervous energy
of line, and assured mark making are entirely Blackadder's own.

## IAN HOWARD
### RSA (b.1952)

Ian Howard is an artist specialising in painting, drawing and printmaking. He is an Academician of the Royal Scottish Academy of Art and Architecture and an Emeritus Professor of the University of Edinburgh. He was formerly Dean of Duncan of Jordanstone College of Art, University of Dundee; a member of the Faculty of the British School at Rome; and the former Principal of Edinburgh College of Art.

His particular research interests include: art and science, alchemical symbolism, hermeticism, emblems, and medieval and renaissance iconography. He lives and works in SW France.

Cat.30, Draco, mixed media on wood panel, 80 x 60 cms.
Exhibited: *First*, The Scottish Gallery, Edinburgh, 2017, cat.16

Draco is essentially an alchemical emblem representing part of the alchemical process. 'Prima Materia' in the course of its elaboration must be subjected to a four-fold division, divided into four elements, described in the form of a cross. This is the cross of Physis, which enables matter to be incarnated and to come into the world. The cross is an allusion to both the conflict of opposites and to the Crucifixion. Only this coming together of opposites can slay the alchemical or mercurial dragon. In alchemy, it is part of the symbolic imagery of 'mortificatio' – killing, decay and decomposition. That which undergoes 'mortificatio' is the 'slaying of the dragon', representing the first elemental state.

## IAN FLEMING
## RSA, RSW (1906–1994)

Fleming was born and schooled in Glasgow and taught
at the Glasgow School of Art from 1931 until 1947.
He was an encouraging teacher who quietly nurtured
the careers of many painters, including the Roberts,
Colquhoun and MacBryde, and Joan Eardley. He moved
to Aberdeen (by way of Hospitalfield House in Arbroath)
and eventually became Head of Painting at Gray's School
of Art. An early love of etching was sustained and in
1987 he showed a series of etchings, his *Thoughts*, at The
Scottish Gallery. In painting, he was an influence on many,
including William Burns, Robert Henderson Blyth and
Joan Eardley.

Cat.31, Nets and Turpaulins,
Lunan Bay, c.1950, oil on canvas,
62 x 76 cms. Exhibited: *The First
150 Years*, The Scottish Gallery,
Edinburgh, 1992

Lunan Bay, which lies between
Arbroath and Montrose, has
attracted many painters to its castle,
sweeping beach and the ruined
limekiln on the headland. Fleming
finds his subject amongst the posts,
parabolas and planes created by
the drying.

## WILLIAM CROSBIE
### (1915–1999)

'My devotion to the muse and the life it has led me has meant I have enjoyed richness of texture not readily to hand to the majority for my fellow citizens.'

Crosbie's mild appraisal of the benefits of having lived a full, creative life rather undersells his contribution. Crosbie is a perfect illustration of how an artist can be a vital part of a school, but whose contribution is so varied and rich that it defies an easy summing up. Guy Peploe wrote the following in the *Centenary Exhibition* catalogue introduction:

There are many Scottish painters who have made a mark on our culture and consciousness in the last century and it is tempting to try to attach each to a school or movement. The artist has a habit of resisting any attempt at taxonomy however, wriggling free from the entomologist's chloroform bottle and display pin, to be unruly, unpredictable and provide no favours for the art historian. Yes, we had The Glasgow Boys, a coherent group of realist painters before the beginning of the 20th Century. And then came The Scottish Colourists, our first modernists, who certainly exhibited as a group and can be understood as British post-impressionists. In the post-War years the choice seemed to be to stay in Scotland under the wing of your Art College or move to the South, like Colquhoun and MacBryde, Alan Davie, William Gear and W. Barns-Graham. Of course the complex reality denies a simple telling; for every adherent there is an opponent and many of the most powerful and individual painters of the period like James Cowie or Joan Eardley neither left nor taught in Glasgow or Edinburgh. The further atomisation and liberalisation of art in its institutions and education from the sixties has led to confusion; the absence

Cat.32, William Crosbie, Butterfly of the Mind, 1990, oil painting, 60.9 x 45.7 cms.
Provenance: The Artist's Estate

of a master and eventual abandonment of the idea, for example, that drawing mattered at all. But of course painting and drawing do matter and we are now in times ripe for the rediscovery of painters who believed this passionately, who dedicated themselves to hard work, sustained by their convictions even when the tide seemed to run against them. William Crosbie was one such. He had a fine, enquiring mind, was deeply read and immersed in the liberal arts; he had great technical gifts and was happy to apply these far beyond the confines of studio and easel but at the same time he recognised that a painter needed to paint and to exhibit. This determination to be engaged with the hurly burly and a prodigious work ethic have left much to be rediscovered and celebrated in the centenary year of his birth.

We have chosen three works to represent Crosbie in this publication. Firstly the studio interior with Jankel Adler, which feeds directly into the next page, is a spirited, typical drawing, still owing something to the School of Paris. The portrait of T. J. Honeyman reminds us of Crosbie's considerable portrait practice, while the subject is a man whose significance in the Scottish art world cannot be overstressed. As a dealer with Reid & Lefevre he was one of the principal supporters of the Scottish Colourists, becoming Hunter's executor and biographer and then writing his Three Scottish Colourists in 1951. As Director of Kelvingrove Art Gallery he oversaw the expansion of the modern and contemporary collections, including the purchase of Salvador Dalí's controversial Christ of St John of the Cross. The third example, *Butterfly of the Mind*, is a beautifully structured and balanced oil painting, which references his lifelong surrealist leanings.

Cat.33, Jankel Adler Talking with Friends in Crosbie's Studio, 1941, ink, 25 x 35 cms. Provenance: The Artist's Estate

Cat.34, Portrait of Dr Tom J. Honeyman, 1945, oil on canvas, 101.5 x 76 cms. Provenance: The Artist's Estate

JOSEF HERMAN
OBE (1911–2000)

Herman had fled first from Warsaw and then Belgium as the war began, coming to Glasgow in 1940 and staying for four years, showing for the first time with The Scottish Gallery in 1942. He was one of many Polish artists, both Catholic and Jewish, who spent time in Scotland, including Jankel Adler. Herman eventually settled in London after a decade in Wales, where he made his reputation with his powerful paintings and drawings of miners. He was a prolific draftsman, arising very early and drawing for hours before breakfast. His subject was always vivid – dancers, animals, lovers, workers – and The Scottish Gallery is planning an exhibition in the Autumn of 2017, drawn from a private collection assembled during the War years.

Another significant Polish emigre artist to settle in Scotland during the war was Aleksander Zyw (1905–1995). Zyw was born in north east Poland, and travelled to Scotland with the reforming Polish Army in 1940. It was in Scotland that he was appointed official war artist and sketched extensively around the camps in Angus and the Borders, before seeing action aboard an Atlantic destroyer and during the Normandy Campaign. The skills he developed from constant sketching enabled Zyw to abandon naturalism in favour of a more subjective and provocative art akin to expressionism. He exhibited at The Scottish Gallery in 1945, and was the Festival exhibitor in 1950 and 1957. Further exhibitions have been held in 2001 and 2012. He was honoured with a retrospective organised by The Scottish Arts Council in 1972 and an exhibition at The Scottish National Gallery of Modern Art entitled *The Nature of Painting* in 1986. Public collections include The Scottish National Gallery of Modern Art and Tate Britain.

Cat.35, Joseph Herman, Ballet Dancers, c.1942, watercolour, 20 x 25.5 cms. Provenance: Private collection, Edinburgh

## COLQUHOUN & MACBRYDE
### (1914–1962) & (1913–1966)

Colquhoun and MacBryde met shortly after enrolling at Glasgow School of Art and soon began the relationship that lasted until Colquhoun's early death aged 47. After graduating from the School in 1937 they both applied for the Annual Travelling Scholarship – its most prestigious award. Although not recognising the true nature of their bonding there was such concern when Colquhoun was ultimately awarded the prize that an equal sum was donated to MacBryde enabling them to tour France, Italy, Belgium and Holland together in 1938 and '39. In 1941, having moved to London, they were loaned a thatched cottage in rural Worcestershire where they produced several oil paintings of landscapes influenced by the Neo-Romantic work of older painters such as Graham Sutherland and John Piper. These helped secure them representation at the prestigious London gallery of Reid and Lefevre. Such was their success with the gallery that they soon became known as 'The Golden Boys of Bond Street'. The Post-Cubist styles that would characterise their work quickly evolved – Colquhoun expressively depicting figures, mostly women, often with animals; MacBryde's work was more decorative, sometimes including a human figure but mostly brightly patterned still lifes.

Although working in assorted media they preferred oil paint for much of their work. After meeting the Polish artist, Jankel Adler in 1943, he showed them how to make monoprints, then an obscure technique where a one-off 'print' is made by transferring a single or multi-coloured image from a smooth surface such as glass or polished stone on to a paper support. Despite becoming increasingly dependent on alcohol in the 1950s, both artists conscientiously worked at their chosen vocation, producing hundreds of artworks in various media. The artistic reputations of 'the two Roberts' which, after their untimely deaths in the 60s, fell into decline, have over the past thirty years, been forcibly re-established and they are now properly considered two outstanding British artists of the mid-twentieth century with works in public collections throughout Britain and abroad.

— © 2014 Roger Bristow. Extract from foreword to The Scottish Gallery exhibition catalogue *Golden Years*, 2014.

The Scottish Gallery first exhibited Colquhoun and Macbryde in 1944. In 2010, The Scottish Gallery curated and produced *The Roberts* to coincide with the monograph *The Last Bohemians* by Roger Bristow. In 2014 The Scottish Gallery presented *Golden Years* which coincided with the retrospective of both artists *The Two Roberts* at the Scottish National Gallery of Modern Art.

Cat.36, Robert MacBryde, European Street Scene
with Stone Archway, 1938, oil on canvas, 35 x 28.5 cms

Opposite: Photograph of Robert MacBryde
and Robert Colquhoun by Felix Man
(1949). Hulton Archive/Getty Images.
Bedford Gardens studio.

Cat.37, Robert Colquhoun, Two Figures No.1, 1953,
carbon transfer and watercolour, 45.5 x 37.5 cms

JOHN BYRNE
RSA (b.1940)

John Byrne was raised in Paisley (including his formative
months as a slab boy at Stoddarts) and attended the Glasgow
School of Art. He was awarded travelling scholarships and
spent time in Italy before coming to Edinburgh to pursue his
studies. Byrne is now regarded as a national treasure and
some settled time in the studio has allowed him to produce
a considerable body of work around the subjects of self-image,
pop culture and gentle fantasy. His genius was always recognised
but it was his rejection of a conventional career as a painter
that led to writing, television and the invention of a naïve alter
ego all designed, with limited success, to avoid himself being the
centre of attention. John Byrne first showed with The Scottish
Gallery in 1973. Further exhibitions have been held in 1992,
1993, 1994, 1995 and 1997.

Cat.38, Night Garden, c.1968, oil on canvas, 71 x 91 cms

Night Garden is an early 'Patrick' painting by John Byrne
(the explanation to the Portal Gallery in London of who had
produced these most sophisticated images was that they were
by his father, uncontactable 'in his beach-hut in Gourock').
Byrne has created a dreamscape borrowed from Douanier
Rousseau, with lolloping rabbits, a rather cross-looking,
reclining siren and a boy and dog who look on with disinterest.

Duncan Shanks drawing beside The River Clyde
at the bottom his garden, February 2017

## DUNCAN SHANKS
### RSA, RSW, RGI (b.1937)

Duncan Shanks was born in Airdrie and studied at
Glasgow School of Art where he later lectured. He
draws his subjects and inspiration from the countryside
around his home in the Clyde Valley. Strong colour and
richly-applied paint chart the changing seasons and
the forces imminent in nature.

'Duncan Shanks is a committed and self-aware
modernist. Nevertheless he chose from the beginning
of his career the apparently old-fashioned idiom of
landscape. It might seem strange to seek to forge a
wholly contemporary art from a form so burdened with
history. It was certainly a struggle. By his own account
he was thirty before he found his true direction as a
painter. That he did do so and has stuck to his chosen
course ever since is a measure of his determination
to meet the challenge he had set himself. As Joan
Eardley did before him, he has since then shown that
it is quite wrong to suppose that landscape cannot
be contemporary. Properly understood, freed from
the burden of imitating the past while nevertheless
confidently learning from it, but also resisting the parallel
pressure to conform to more transient modes of
making art, he has shown that it can be as modern
and relevant as any art form.'

— Duncan Macmillan, Quoted from foreword to
*Winter Journey* exhibition catalogue, 2017

The Dying Sun, acrylic on paper, 62.5 x 121 cms.
Exhibited: *Duncan Shanks, Winter Journey*, The Scottish Gallery, Edinburgh, 2017, cat. 26

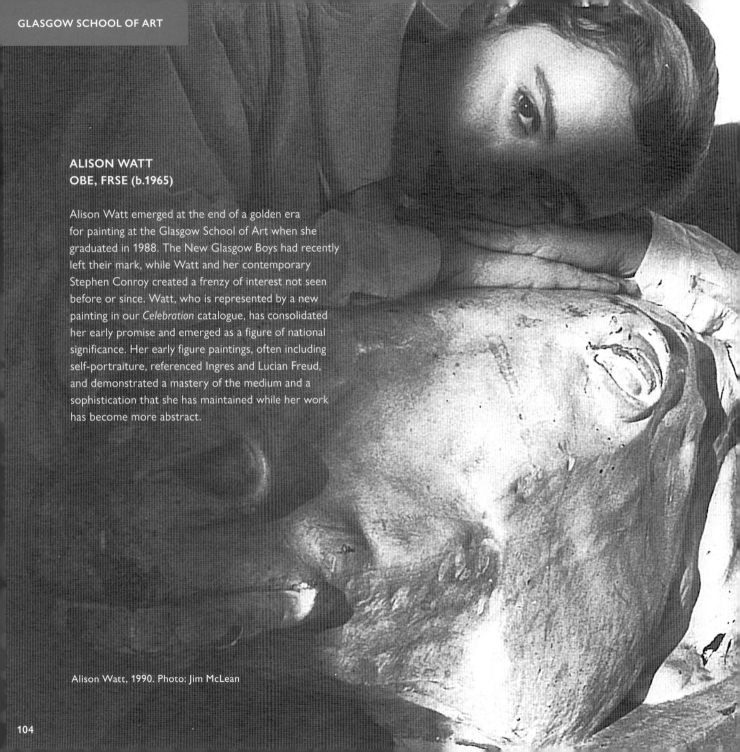

## ALISON WATT
### OBE, FRSE (b.1965)

Alison Watt emerged at the end of a golden era for painting at the Glasgow School of Art when she graduated in 1988. The New Glasgow Boys had recently left their mark, while Watt and her contemporary Stephen Conroy created a frenzy of interest not seen before or since. Watt, who is represented by a new painting in our *Celebration* catalogue, has consolidated her early promise and emerged as a figure of national significance. Her early figure paintings, often including self-portraiture, referenced Ingres and Lucian Freud, and demonstrated a mastery of the medium and a sophistication that she has maintained while her work has become more abstract.

Alison Watt, 1990. Photo: Jim McLean

The Last Supper, 1988, oil on canvas, 61 x 61 cms.
Provenance: Private Collection, Edinburgh

The Gallery first exhibited Alison's work shortly after she graduated from Glasgow School of Art in 1988 and was closely associated with her at this time. Her first solo exhibition was held at The Scottish Gallery, London in 1990 to wide critical acclaim and was subsequently seen at Kelvingrove Museum and Art Gallery. Her public collections include the Scottish National Gallery of Modern Art, Edinburgh, Glasgow Art Gallery and Museum, National Portrait Gallery, London and the Uffizi Collection, Florence.

## ALBERTO MORROCCO
### OBE, FRSA, FRSE, RSW, RGI (1917–1998)

Alberto Morrocco was born to immigrant parents in Aberdeen, where he would attend Gray's School of Art. After the difficult war years, when he was briefly interned as an enemy alien in Edinburgh Castle, he moved in 1950 to teach at Duncan of Jordanstone College of Art and Design in Dundee, where he eventually became Head of Painting. Morrocco is principally associated with the college, although he never lost his delightful Italian-Aberdeen accent.

His ebullient personality was reflected in his department and he recruited artists such as Jack Knox, James Morrison, David McClure and Peter Collins to his staff. His difficult relationship with James McIntosh Patrick (known as Jimmy Patrick) lent colour to staff meetings. One year, tutors were invited to his studio just after the Easter holiday to be greeted with a sumptuous Italian spread and invited to celebrate Leonardo da Vinci's birthday!

His growing family and wife, Vera, provided early intimiste subjects, often in the splendid setting of Binrock, the family home. He returned to Italy on many occasions and found inspiration on the beaches of the riviera and Sicily (as well as North Africa), painting bathers, melon sellers, glimpsed interiors, donkeys, dogs and boys. In his studio he mastered still life, often fancifully enhanced with a harlequin figure, and increasingly used brilliant colour, replacing his earlier, typically tonal constructions with direct expressionist works which became hugely popular.

In 2017, his centenary year, The Scottish Gallery is delighted to mount an exhibition for the Edinburgh International Festival to celebrate his life and unique contribution to Scottish painting.

Alberto Morrocco, 1996. Photo: Chris Close

Cat.39, Alberto Morrocco, The Sicilian Cart, oil on board, 56 x 85 cms. Exhibited: *Centenary Exhibition*, The Scottish Gallery, Edinburgh, 2017. Provenance: Collection of Roy and Mairi Rankin, Edinburgh. Literature: *Alberto Morrocco* by Victoria Keller and Clara Young, 1993, p.37

## DAVID MCCLURE
### RSA, RSW (1926–1998)

David McClure was born in Glasgow and attended
Edinburgh College of Art, but is primarily associated
with Dundee. He was ten years junior to Alberto
Morrocco, but a close friend and colleague; together,
their emphasis on *belle peinture*, strong colour and
their instinctive ability as picture-makers lent a strong
character to their contributions to college life and
the many group and annual exhibitions in which they
participated together. McClure's most direct Scottish
influences however were Gillies, Redpath and the
Edinburgh School; he painted with Anne Redpath and
Hamish Reid on more than one occasion and his work
on paper owes much to Gillies, just as the whimsy
and poetry of his subject pictures owes something
to John Maxwell.

David McClure painting on the Terrace, Florence, 1956

Cat.40, Figures and Flowers, 1963, oil on canvas, 76 x 63.5 cms.

Exhibited: *The First 150 Years*, The Scottish Gallery, Edinburgh, 1992

*Figures and Flowers* is a fine example of the work influenced by
Maxwell and Chagall, incorporating still life, fantasy and the figure.

## JAMES MORRISON
### RSA, RSW (b.1932)

James Morrison was born in Glasgow and attended the School
of Art from 1950–1954. His first subject was the City of
Glasgow, the cleared spaces, derelict tenements and brooding
Victorian terraces of the West End. In this era of real austerity
there was a deeply conservative establishment and young artists
felt the need to come together and make their own exhibiting
opportunities, outwith the academies and institutions. He was
a founder member of The Glasgow Group, showed with the
McClure Gallery in Glasgow and most importantly began his
long, fruitful relationship with The Scottish Gallery with his first
solo show in 1958. By 1960, married and looking for a fresh
start he moved to the Kincardineshire coast, first at Catterline
and then Montrose from 1965 when he began lecturing at
Duncan of Jordanstone College of Art, Dundee, where he
was to remain until a contract with The Gallery allowed him
to retire and paint full time from 1987.

The rich farmland of Angus with the Grampians beyond, the
farmsteads, field structures, hedgerows and beech trees and
above all the ever-changing, towering skies, became his subject.
In *Legaston Farm* we sense a perfectly still day in early spring,
the tall repoussoir in the foreground still 'without their clothes'
the land falling gently down to a farm, settled behind its stand
of trees with the land rising again behind.

Opposite: Cat.41, Legaston Farm, 15.11.86, oil on board, 89 x 122 cms.
Provenance: The Scottish Gallery, Edinburgh; Private collection, Edinburgh

## ALAN ROBB
### RSW, RSA (b.1946)

Alan Robb was born in Glasgow and brought up in
Aberdeen. He was awarded his Diploma in Art from
Grays School of Art in 1968 and after a further year
of Post Graduate study at Gray's, gained a place in the
Painting School of the Royal College of Art, graduating
in 1972. Robb was appointed assistant art master at
Oundle School in Northamptonshire and in 1975,
relocated to Cork as painting tutor at the Crawford
School of Art. In 1980 he became head of Diploma
Studies and as well as Painting, Printmaking and
Sculpture, his remit included Art History, Stained Glass
and Violin making. In 1983 he was appointed Head of
the School of Fine Art at Duncan of Jordanstone
College of Art, Dundee and was awarded a personal
chair in 1989. He was elected a member of the Royal
Scottish Society of Painters in Watercolour in 2010
and a member of the Royal Scottish Academy in 2011.

Robb is interested in religious iconography and
artifacts. The removal of context and recreation in
two dimensions heightens any inherent ambiguity
in his subject. This heightening of artistic distance,
the opposite of expressionism, allows religiosity and
kitsch, pathos and humour, spirituality and crudity to
coexist in a world that the artist makes deliberately
resistant to direct interpretation.

Alan Robb in his studio, Newport on Tay, 2016. Photo: Bruce Pert

Cat.42, San Donino Chapel, 2004, oil on linen, 60 x 60 cms.
Exhibited: *First*, The Scottish Gallery, Edinburgh, 2017, cat.41

## PHILIP BRAHAM (b.1959)

Phil Braham is both a painter and photographer, a conceptual artist who uses oil paint as his usual medium. He was a Dundee graduate who showed first with The Scottish Gallery in 1985, powerful expressionist works referencing both violent personal experience and abstract recreations of the battlefield. His work was included in *The Vigorous Imagination*, a significant survey exhibition of contemporary Scottish art in 1987. His philosophical engagement with the history of light and dark, of place, of legend, of real events and their resonances continues today, but his approach has moved towards realism. He has taught part-time at Duncan of Jordanstone since 2000 and led a course in Painting and Philosophy since 2013.

Philip Braham in his studio, 2016.

Opposite: Cat.43, Psalm, 2016, oil on canvas, 61 x 46 cms. Exhibited: *Flora Depicta*, The Scottish Gallery, July 2016, cat.4

## JAMES COWIE
### RSA (1886–1956)

James Cowie is often cited as the best example of
a painter who defies easy analysis in terms of school.
He attended Gray's School of Art in Aberdeen,
worked in schools, most notably at Bellshill Academy
in Lanarkshire, was one of the most distinguished
wardens of the Patrick Allan-Fraser School of Art
at Hospitalfield House in Arbroath and then retired
to Edinburgh.

Hospitalfield, a country house which can lay claim to
be the oldest art school in Scotland, has its origin as
a religious building in the thirteenth century. Its modern
history spans from 1890 when its owner, the arts
patron Patrick Allan-Fraser died and endowed its future
for 'the promotion of Education in the Arts'. Many
artists have benefited from its unique atmosphere,
traditions and collections, including The Roberts,
Joan Eardley, Peter Howson and Callum Innes. Eardley
famously did not see eye to eye with Cowie, but his
emphasis on the primacy of drawing and advocacy of
the importance of painting in the modern world must
have been an influence.

His own drawing and painting, distinguished by his
brilliant, close observation of character which lent his
figure compositions a particular poignancy, is often
presented in a disquieting setting where uncertainties
of scale and strange juxtapositions undermine a
conventional reading.

Above: The Blue Shirt, 1945–50, oil on canvas, 66 x 55.5 cms.
University of Edinburgh Fine Art Collection

Opposite, top: Cat.44, In the Country 1930, watercolour, 22 x 23 cms, Exhibited: Royal Scottish Academy, Edinburgh, 1953; *James Cowie, Memorial Exhibition*, The Arts Council Scottish Committee, Traveling exhibition, 1957, cat.53; *James Cowie – Enigmata*, The Scottish Gallery, Edinburgh, June 2015, cat. 14

Opposite, bottom: Cat.45, Book Leaves, 1935, mixed media, 28 x 35.5 cms. Exhibited: Royal Scottish Academy, Edinburgh, 1953; *James Cowie, Memorial Exhibition*, The Arts Council Scottish Committee, Traveling exhibition, 1957, cat.75; *Recent Acquisitions*, The Scottish Gallery, Edinburgh, 1977, cat.30; *James Cowie – Enigmata*, The Scottish Gallery, Edinburgh, June 2015, cat. 14

## WILLIAM BURNS
### RSA, RSW, RI (1921–1972)

William Burns is another Glasgow born and trained painter who made his life and reputation in Aberdeen, tutoring at Gray's School of Art. The influence of Ian Fleming is apparent in his earlier work, but like his contemporary and colleague Robert Henderson Blyth his work shifted towards the abstract as European influences of tachism and Nicolas de Staël came to bear. For Burns, a passion for flying lent a different aspect to his vision; like Peter Lanyon in Cornwall, the coast seen from above was his great inspiration in later work, and like the Englishman he sadly met his death in a flying accident.

Cat.46, A Terrace, 1948, oil on canvas, 76 x 101.5 cms. Exhibited: *Modern Masters VI*, The Scottish Gallery, Edinburgh, January 2017, cat.16. Provenance: Private collection

Cat.47, The Sea Wall, c.1960, oil on board, 70 x 105 cms. Exhibited: *Modern Masters VI*,
The Scottish Gallery, Edinburgh, January 2017, cat.15. Provenance: Private collection

Alexander Fraser ©GF Images

## ALEXANDER FRASER
### RSA, RSW (b.1940)

'A renowned portrait painter with works in many public and private collections, Sandy's versatility as an artist is evident in his incorporating and mixing numerous elements including traditional portraiture, abstraction and representational landscape genres into his dreamlike paintings. Utilising a flat plane, vignettes tell stories and suggest situations to keep our eyes moving and our thoughts turning as to what is happening in these large-scale works. A window into the working practice of a master painter.'

— Taken from the text accompanying his exhibition in 2015 at the RSA *Muchalls Folk Art*.

As head of the painting school at Gray's in Aberdeen until his retirement in 2007, Fraser has been an enormous influence on many painters like Jo Fan, Joyce W. Cairns and Barry McGlashan, and while his own early work is largely abstract, his persistent drawing, acute observational powers and vivid internal visual life produced an Aberdonian magic realism which is one aspect of the continuing relevance of painting in Scotland.

Opposite: How High the Moon, 2010, oil on canvas, 213 x 152 cms. Exhibited: *New Paintings*, The Scottish Gallery, Edinburgh, 2011, cat.1

## WILLIAM JOHNSTONE
## (1897–1981)

William Johnstone, c.1980.
Photo: James Gardiner

In this chapter *The Painting Schools of Scotland* we have been at pains to stress the fallibility of a coherent concept, the never-ending cross-fertilization of the institutions and the reaction against authority (as represented by an art school) which is the normal course of education. Many Scottish artists have gone further afield and have attended art schools across the border, particularly for postgraduate study. William Johnstone, who came from the Scottish Borders, was a graduate of Edinburgh College of Art who made his professional life in London, firstly at Camberwell and then as Principal of Central School of Arts and Crafts from 1947 to 1960. Here, as an inspirational leader, he encouraged the Edinburgh graduates Alan Davie and Eduardo Paolozzi to come and study. Unlike these two, Johnstone returned to Scotland, to run the family farm near Selkirk. While he became prolific and ambitious in scale, his adherence to the abstract form absolute (albeit inspired by the Borders landscape) he did not enjoy the compliments of the Scottish art establishment he might have expected and became a somewhat isolated figure.

The Scottish Gallery brought this artist back from isolation in 2012 with the critically acclaimed exhibition *Marchlands* which was the catalyst for a new audience and further academic research.

Public Collections include:
National Portrait Gallery, London
Tate Gallery, London
The Fleming Collection, London
University of Edinburgh
National Galleries of Scotland
Scottish National Gallery of Modern Art, Edinburgh
Dundee Art Galleries & Museums Collection

Self Portrait, 1978, oil on canvas, 76 x 63 cms.
Exhibited: *William Johnstone, Marchlands*, The Scottish
Gallery, Edinburgh, 2012. Purchased by The Hope Scott
Trust for The Scottish National Portrait Gallery, 2012.

Self Portrait is from a series of five painted in 1978.
One was in the collection of Camberwell School of Art
and is now presumed lost. There is no stylistic compromise
in the self-depiction, rather, as in all his best work, the
swift constructive and destructive mark-making reveal the
truth and essence of the subject; worn-out but resilient,
disappointed but triumphant.

'To some of Johnstone's staff at Camberwell and the
Central, and others in other walks of life who have
encountered him, he has seemed a dreamer and a mystic.
In earlier life such an impression was offset by an intense
practicality. But in later life he is able to dream and, in
the manner of old men, to review his past life.'
— Douglas Hall, 1980

Cat.48, William Johnstone, Countryside in Wartime-Broomhill, 1923, oil on board, 73.7 x 63.5 cms.
Exhibited: *South America Fine Arts*, 1943; Museo Provincial de Bellas Artes, Cordoba, Argentina; Museu Nacional de Bellas Artes, Rio de Janeiro, Brazil; Arts Council of Great Britain, London, William Johnstone, 1981, cat.4; *William Johnstone (1897–1981) A Centenary Celebration*, Talbot Rice Gallery, 1997; *Modern Masters*, The Scottish Gallery, Edinburgh, 2013. Provenance: The Stafford Gallery, London; with Alex Reid & Lefevre, London

Cat.49, William Johnstone, Untitled, Geometric, 1975, ink brush drawing, 76 x 56 cms

### EARL HAIG
### OBE, RSA (1918–2009)

Dawyck Haig became a student under the watchful eye of William Johnstone at Camberwell School of Art in 1945. The son of Field Marshal Douglas Haig, he inevitably lived his life in his father's shadow, the accusation that he was a dilettante a constant (if unspoken) rebuke. His persistence and the rehabilitation of his father's reputation as a military commander allowed him the satisfaction of late success. A consistent supporter was The Scottish Gallery, with whom he enjoyed an unbroken relationship following his release from Colditz Castle at the end of the Second World War, including the display of his POW sketches in 1945 and a triumphant exhibition for his ninetieth birthday in 2009.

Dawyck Haig is now routinely considered as a painter who made a significant contribution to Scottish painting over seventy years. His engagement with the landscape of the Borders, around the family estate at Bemersyde and his love affair with Venice produced distinct bodies of work which have been celebrated in his 16 shows with The Gallery.

Left: Portrait of Earl Haig at 75

Cat.50, Santa Maria Formosa, oil on canvas, 61 x 91.5 cms. Exhibited: *Memorial Exhibition*,
The Scottish Gallery, 2011, cat.1. Provenance: Private Collection, Edinburgh

# / FIVE /

# Modern Scottish Women

# Modern Scottish Women

Many observers of the art world have remarked at how male-dominated it seems. If one starts out from the premise that both sexes are equally creative then the fault has to lie with glass ceilings and patriarchal historians. No named artists survive from pre-antiquity, and few, all male, from classical times. When Vasari published his *Lives of the Artists* in 1550, recognised as the first work of art history, women were left unnoticed. In the modern period, we have new measures of visibility: inclusions in collections and exhibitions and measures of popularity in an era when we consume art like any other commodity. In the last hundred years, as impediments were removed, many social pressures persisted and we have to congratulate many of the great women artists of the last century on their dedication as well as their genius. In the generally strong area of Modern British art (in art world parlance, if you have died you are 'modern' and if you survive you are 'contemporary'), sculptors like Barbara Hepworth still lag behind Henry Moore, and Elisabeth Frink represents the women in the second rank, below Lynn Chadwick, Anthony Caro and Michael Ayrton. The painters are even further behind – or, in the logic of a potential investor, the women have more potential. While Lucian Freud and Francis Bacon occupy an international stratosphere, permanently in the top ten, painters like Prunella Clough, Joan Eardley and Anne Redpath are well adrift of the values achieved by William Scott, Patrick Caulfield or Ivon Hitchens. In Edinburgh, the Scottish National Gallery of Modern Art has gone some way to addressing the historic deficit, with Alice Strang's exhibition *Modern Scottish Women: Painters and Sculptors 1885–1965* (7 November 2015 to 26 June 2016).

A glance at our programme for our 175th anniversary year sees a perfect balance of the sexes and, significantly, Kate Downie being our Festival exhibitor. The Scottish Gallery has been a champion of women artists for decades, not to fulfil any quota or gender equality 'policy' – we have championed women because the work was valid. It is less than one hundred years ago that women were allowed the vote. In the first half of the last century, art education was in effect only available to the upper classes, and a career as an artist was routinely

> The Scottish Gallery has been a champion of women artists for decades, not to fulfil any quota or gender equality 'policy' – we have championed women because the work was valid.

Previous: Nets, Waves and Rocks, c.1961, oil and collage on hardboard, 69 x 91 cms. Exhibited: *Festival Exhibition*, The Scottish Gallery, Edinburgh, 1964, cat.14; *Joan Eardley*, The Scottish Gallery, 2013, cat.8. Provenance: The artist's studio inventory (ED 157). Sold by The Gallery, 2013

Anne Redpath with fellow students
at Edinburgh College of Art, c.1915.
Courtesy of the artist's estate

131

Top: Joan Eardley, Summer 1961, Catterline, 1961.
Photo: Audrey Walker

Bottom: Scottish Society of Women Artists Exhibition
in RSA Galleries – Miss Perpetua Pope – Mrs F Lauglin
and Miss Anne Redpath, c.1960 © The Scotsman
Publications Ltd. Licensor www.scran.ac.uk

curtailed, for women, by marriage and children.
Post WWI, radical social change took place and art
education became more readily available to those from
different classes and backgrounds, but women artists
still struggled to survive. In the post-War period, a
succession of great women artists have underpinned our
programme, supported by many dozens of others, many
showing multiple times. Anne Redpath, in particular, was
outward in her gaze, partly because of the necessity
to make her way as a professional artist while mother
to three young boys through the difficult war years,
living back in the Borders after more than ten years in
France. In the war's aftermath her star rose rapidly; the
beginning of the Edinburgh International Festival and the
wealth of exhibiting opportunities that emerged in the
fifties in Edinburgh, London, and Bristol, as well as with
the Arts Council of Great Britain, saw Redpath in the
vanguard. She was the direct descendant of the Scottish
Colourists, Peploe in particular, as she demonstrated
her extraordinary facility, colour sense and unerring
choice of subject. Latterly her curiosity and adventure
found painterly fulfilment in long trips to continental
Europe, initially back to the France she knew so well
from the twenties, but then to Spain, Venice, Portugal
and the Canaries. This adventure was always put to
good use, with sketchbooks filled and objects found and
brought back to the studio to enrich her iconography.
In later years she was able to respond to developments
in international painting by moving towards an undefined
picture space in which her flowers and vases merge into
backgrounds built up with the vigour and élan of Nicolas
de Staël or Antoni Tàpies.

Joan Eardley also found opportunities unavailable to a
previous generation in the fifties and sixties, not least
with The Scottish Gallery, and in the more than fifty
years since her death we have continued to represent

FOUR WOMEN ARTISTS

ELIZABETH BLACKADDER

VICTORIA CROWE

ALISON MᶜGILL

EMILY SUTTON

4ᵗʰ ~ 25ᵗʰ November
2015

THE SCOTTISH GALLERY

Exhibition catalogue for *Four Women Artists*, November 2015. Cover design by Emily Sutton. Exhibition coincided w
exhibition at the Scottish National Gallery of Modern Art *Modern Scottish Women – Painters and Sculptors 1885-*

Elizabeth Blackadder, Gladioli, 2011, oil on canvas, 101 x 76 cms.

Exhibited: *Elizabeth Blackadder, Festival Exhibition*, The Scottish Gallery, Edinburgh, 2011, cat. 22

her estate and promote her national and international reputation. Her only commissioned work is the portrait of Bill Macaulay's children (seen on p.17). The power of her work to engage and move the viewer is undimmed; her twin subjects of Glasgow and Catterline are now rediscovered by new generations, her poignant story retold and better understood.

Over the last forty years or so, Dame Elizabeth Blackadder, Barbara Rae and Victoria Crowe have emerged as three of Scotland's most eloquent and significant painters, their work fresh, original and widely appreciated. Blackadder, well known in the capital through her membership of the Royal Academy, was a senior tutor at Edinburgh College of Art and has been lauded with honours, degrees and retrospectives. Her painting in watercolour and oil and her prodigious oeuvre of printmaking are marked by a restraint and delicacy which still deliver arresting strength. Rae is also a RA, a brilliant colourist who has found her landscape inspiration in Southern Spain and Western Ireland as well as closer to home, and produces textured paintings with saturated and luminous colour that exists in the consciousness between real and recalled experience. Victoria Crowe, who came to Edinburgh from London in the early seventies, like the other two has found inspiration in travel (she has a second home in Venice), but much of her inspiration is internal, or springs from text and ephemera, nature and the built environment. Her sensitivity to time of day, to texture and to surface has led to a layered approach in picture-making unique in contemporary practice, which has brought her wide and deep appreciation. She is our Festival exhibitor next year (2018), when she also has a portrait retrospective at the Scottish National Portrait Gallery.

Anne Redpath exhibition invitation, The Scottish Gallery, 1957

## ANNE REDPATH
### OBE, RSA, ARA, RWA (1895–1965)

Anne Redpath was the pivotal figure in the group of painters now referred to as the Edinburgh School. She attended the Edinburgh College of Art, receiving her diploma in 1917. After a lengthy spell in the South of France, Redpath returned to Hawick in the mid 1930s. Her brilliant manipulation of paint, left in delicious peaks or eked across a rough surface with a palette knife, is characteristic of her varied responses to different subjects at different times. In the last years of her output she often favoured a limited palette – perhaps a few brilliant, jewel-like notes enlivening a dark or white composition.

Redpath was an inspirational person and formed many enduring friendships. Her flat in London Street became an artistic salon, celebrated by Robin Philipson's famous, affectionate group portrait in The Scottish National Portrait Gallery. She had considerable commercial success in her lifetime, enjoying a fruitful, consistent relationship with The Scottish Gallery and latterly with Reid & Lefevre in London. Since her passing, her reputation has been further enhanced with retrospective and centenary exhibitions, so that now she is established as one of the great figures in twentieth-century Scottish painting.

Opposite: Cat.51, Pink House, Corsica, c.1954, oil on board, 50.6 x 61 cms. Exhibited: *A Dozen Paintings and Works on Paper*, The Scottish Gallery, Edinburgh, 2016, cat. 5. Provenance: Melrose's Tea c.1990, The Scottish Gallery, Edinburgh

"Each new landscape and culture that Redpath encountered changed and informed not only the landscapes and architectural subjects she produced but also everything she painted thereafter including her still lifes. In Corsica in 1954 and in Gran Canaria in 1959 she experienced harsh sun-bleached hillsides where the resulting paintings the houses appear as though they grow out of the hills, giving them a 'buttress-like presence'. Simultaneously she suggests erosion, decay and permanence." – *Blue Sky on a Grey Day*, written by Patrick Bourne for *Anne Redpath, Fifty*, The Scottish Gallery, July 2015, page 7

Anne Redpath in her London Street flat, Edinburgh, 1960 © The Scotsman Publications Ltd. Licensor www.scran.ac.uk

Cat.52, Anne Redpath, The White Azalea, c.1963, oil on canvas,
51 x 61 cms. Exhibited: *Anne Redpath, Fifty*, The Scottish Gallery,
Edinburgh, 2015, cat. 32; *Anne Redpath, A Dozen Paintings*,
The Scottish Gallery, 2016, cat.11. Provenance: The Artist's Family

## JOAN EARDLEY
### RSA (1921–1963)

There is an enduring fascination for Joan Eardley far beyond her unconventional life and early death at the age of forty-two. Born in 1921 in Sussex, Joan Eardley's family moved to Scotland in 1939 and a year later she joined the Glasgow School of Art. She found subjects in the shipyards of Clydebank and the slums of Townhead, at first the rundown tenements and buildings and later the children and street life around the maternity hospital on Rottenrow, where the character of the people and the place became the vital subject of her work. Her art education was finished with scholarship visits to Paris and the cities of Renaissance Italy. However, by the fifties Joan Eardley divided her life between her studio in Townhead and the fishing village of Catterline in the north-east of Scotland. Eardley felt at ease in these two contrasting localities, and over the succeeding decade, as if by accident, she created an epic vision of the world from no more than two streets and one small fishing hamlet. The slums of Townhead are no more, the harsh realities and the spirit of the people memorialised by the honesty of her vision, enduring like no other example in the history of Scottish art. Catterline remains unchanged and the village is inevitably a place of pilgrimage for the thousands who admire the artist's deep-felt engagement with nature on the Kincardineshire coast.

Joan Eardley was a regular gallery exhibitor during her lifetime and The Scottish Gallery has become rightly associated with the artist after her death, especially in the last ten years. In 2007, the National Galleries mounted the first major Joan Eardley exhibition in twenty years. Her work filled the palatial rooms of the Royal Scottish Academy building; it was a remarkable, seminal exhibition, which brought the full force of her

talent back into the public arena, and interest in the artist and her work has grown ever since. The Scottish Gallery also hosted a Joan Eardley exhibition in 2007, which took five years of planning and resulted in one of the most successful exhibitions The Gallery has ever held. In 2013, The Scottish Gallery in conjunction with the Portland Gallery, London opened an exhibition to mark the fiftieth anniversary of Joan Eardley's death, coinciding with the publication of a new monograph by Christopher Andreae. In 2017, The Gallery held the exhibition *Restless Talent* to coincide with a new retrospective exhibition at the Scottish National Gallery of Modern Art, *A Sense of Place*.

Above: Joan Eardley in her Townhead Studio, c.1959. Photo: Audrey Walker

Opposite: Joan Eardley exhibition catalogues. From left: *Joan Eardley*, April 2013; *Joan Eardley, In Context*, August 2015; *Joan Eardley, Restless Talent*, February 2017

Above: Cat.53, Joan Eardley, Boy Sleeping in Blue, c.1962, pastel on glass paper, 22 x 28 cms. Exhibited: *Old and Modern Paintings*, Roland, Browse and Delbanco, London, as *Sleeping Boy in Blue*, cat. 1; *Joan Eardley, Restless Talent*, The Scottish Gallery, Edinburgh, 2017, cat.9. Provenance: The artist's studio inventory number ED838; Mercury Gallery, Edinburgh, 1986

The opportunity of a child falling asleep would not have been missed by an artist whose subject was otherwise in perpetual motion, and there are several pastels of this sleeping infant, two illustrated on p.123 of Christopher Andreae's book. In our drawing the little boy's face is squished up, his mouth open where a new tooth catches the light. The brilliant, saturated blue of his top and the light catching the short hair on the back of his head, as well as his ruddy cheeks, make a strong colour statement.

Opposite: Children and Chalked Wall, c.1962, mixed media on paper, 36 x 56 cms (detail). Exhibited: *Joan Eardley*, The Scottish Gallery, 2013, cat. 30. Sold by The Gallery, 2013

## WILHELMINA BARNS-GRAHAM
## CBE, HRSA, HRSW (1912–2004)

Wilhelmina Barns-Graham, known as Willie, was born in
St Andrews, Fife, on 8 June 1912. Determining while at school
that she wanted to be an artist, she set her sights on Edinburgh
College of Art, where she enrolled in 1932 and graduated
with her diploma in 1937. At the suggestion of the College's
principal, Hubert Wellington, she moved to St Ives in 1940.
Early on she met Borlase Smart, Alfred Wallis and Bernard
Leach, as well as Ben Nicholson, Barbara Hepworth and Naum
Gabo who were living locally at Carbis Bay. Her peers in
St Ives include, among others, Patrick Heron, Terry Frost,
Roger Hilton, and John Wells. Barns-Graham's history is bound
up with St Ives, where she lived throughout her life. In 1951
she won the Painting Prize in the Penwith Society of Arts in
Cornwall Festival of Britain Exhibition and went on to have
her first London solo exhibition at the Redfern Gallery in 1952.
She was included in many of the important exhibitions on
pioneering British abstract art that took place in the 1950s.

In 1960, Barns-Graham inherited Balmungo House near
St Andrews, which initiated a new phase in her life. From
this moment she divided her time between the two coastal
communities, establishing herself as a Scottish artist as much
as a St Ives one. Important exhibitions of her work at the
Tate St Ives in 1999/2000 and 2005, and the publication of
the first monograph on her life and work, Lynne Green's
*W. Barns-Graham: A Studio Life*, 2001 confirmed her as one of
the key contributors of the St Ives School, and as a significant
British modernist. She died in St Andrews on 26 January 2004.

Photo: Wilhelmina Barns-Graham exhibition at The Scottish Gallery, 1981 (George Street premises).
Photograph courtesy of the Wilhelmina Barns-Graham Trust

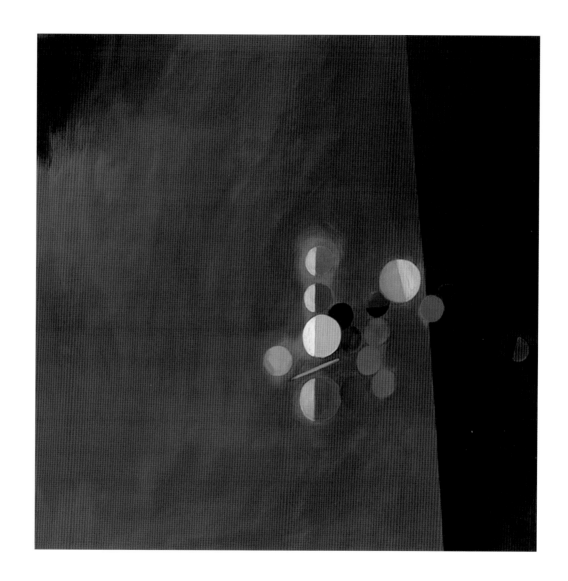

Cat.54, Movement in Space Days Nights, 1980, oil on canvas, 101.5 x 102.2 cms.
Provenance: The Wilhelmina Barns-Graham Trust Inventory no. BGT431

'In the 1990s, while in her 80s, Barns-Graham's paintings became more freely painted, demonstrating an urgency from within the artist. *The Scorpio Series*, as it was called, introduced her paintings to new audiences and revitalised her career. The strong colour and dynamic movement of the images reveal a joie de vivre that communicates itself strongly with the viewer.'

— Geoffrey Bertram,
The Wilhelmina Barns-Graham Trust

Opposite: Cat.55, Scorpio Series 2, No.15, 1996, acrylic on paper, 56.5 x 76 cms. Exhibited: *Modern Masters III*, The Scottish Gallery, Edinburgh, 2014, cat.2; *Last Light*, The Scottish Gallery, 2016, cat. 7. Provenance: The Wilhelmina Barns-Graham Trust Inventory no. BGT944

*Scorpio Series 2* is recognised as being one of the most important series of her career. This is a vibrant painting – an explosion of colour and form which confronts the senses and is painted with absolute certainty. In 1996, the Scottish National Gallery of Modern Art held a retrospective of her work and this picture is a reflection of the artistic confidence in her own abilities and position.

Wilhelmina Barns-Graham portrait, 2001.
Photo: Rowan James

Cat.56, Wilhelmina Barns-Graham, Movement on Brown, 1960, gouache, 53.5 x 42 cms.
Exhibited: *W. Barns-Graham Exhibition*, The Scottish Gallery, Edinburgh, 1960, cat.20. Provenance: Private collection, Midlothian

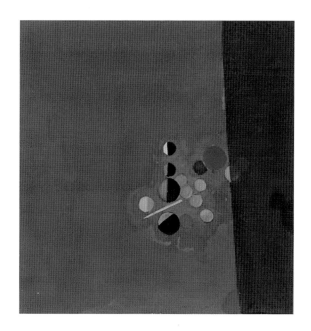

Cat.57, Wilhelmina Barns-Graham, Movement in Space (Into Brown), 1980, gouache,
24.8 x 24.8 cms. Provenance: The Wilhelmina Barns-Graham Trust Inventory no. BGT1059

# ELIZABETH BLACKADDER
## DBE, RA, RSA, RSW, RGI (b.1931)

In considering the last hundred and twenty or so years of Scottish art, the period broadly covering the modern and of course the contemporary (those artists who enjoy the distinction of still being with us), we can detect commonalities: those that spring from a consideration of the same landscapes for example, or those to do with the enjoyment of the medium of oil paint. This allows us to make comparison between Peploe, Redpath and Eardley or George Leslie Hunter, MacTaggart and John Houston.

Creativity is as messy as nature and there is no unbroken line of development, indeed the notion of development has become invalid: modernism has provided the liberty to the artist to make work out of anything and depict anything and the art world has become atomised. For more than half of this period the images of Elizabeth Blackadder have surprised and beguiled us, a presence that has grown and achievements that can be considered as quite discrete from the usual fodder for the survey of our national school. She can perhaps best be considered as a national treasure, like Burns or Scott or Raeburn, her body of work a monument to quiet application, restraint, enlightenment and cultural variety. Each work has the simple poetry of a haiku but is presented with the perfect pitch of a tuning fork.

We have celebrated a consistent relationship between the artist and Gallery, having held ten exhibitions, the last six coinciding with the Edinburgh Festival, put on with The Scottish Gallery. Of course she has shown elsewhere, not least with the National Galleries of Scotland and her long association with the Royal Academy (she became an Associate in 1971 and was the first woman to be a member of both the RA and RSA) has added to her national profile. The list of honours and exhibitions runs to a book in itself and it is hard to grasp the breadth of her achievement across many media. For many she is best understood as a watercolourist, for many more her printmaking has allowed collectors to own her work, new editions of etchings, screen prints and lithographs appearing regularly. Blackadder, like several Edinburgh School painters, has maintained separate watercolour and oil studios. Her compositions in oil must be seen as her greatest contribution, brilliant fusions of real objects and imaginary space, limitless colour invention moderated by impeccable combination, the perfect balance of sharp focus and free drawing with the brush and an unerring sense of restraint and harmony, never overworked.

Guy Peploe

Elizabeth Blackadder, 2003. Photo: Norman McBeath. Courtesy of National Portrait Gallery, London

Cat.58, The Yellow Table, 1976, oil on canvas, 76 x 122 cms.
Exhibited: Elizabeth Blackadder – *Decades, Browse & Darby*,
London, 2015, cat. 7; *Elizabeth Blackadder – Decades*,
The Scottish Gallery, Edinburgh, 2016, cat. 12

Flowers are often present in Elizabeth Blackadder's still-life
compositions and increasingly they became a subject in themselves.
She acquired her first garden with her move to Queen's Crescent
in 1963. There can be no other painter so prolific as regards the
number of things included in her painting: toys, wrappers, ceramics,
postcards, fabric, fruit (real and carved), boxes, bowls, parcels
and so on. When she travelled she accumulated things and then,
eventually, they might be put to use, often crumpled, upside down,
rescaled, flattened or partial.

## PAT DOUTHWAITE
## (1934–2002)

Pat Douthwaite was born in Glasgow in 1934. She began to study mime and modern dance with Margaret Morris, whose husband, J.D. Fergusson, encouraged her to paint. This important influence apart, she was self-taught. In 1958, Pat lived in Suffolk with a group of painters, including the Scots Robert Colquhoun, Robert MacBryde and William Crozier. From 1959 to 1988 she travelled widely, to North Africa, India, Peru, Venezuela, Europe, the USA, Kashmir, Nepal, Pakistan, Ecuador, and from 1969 she lived part of the time in Majorca, before moving to various properties across the Scottish Borders.

She died in July 2002 at Broughty Ferry. Pat Douthwaite is one of the most distinctive artists of the post-war period. She was recently included in the Scottish National Gallery of Modern Art's exhibition *Modern Scottish Women: Painters and Sculptors 1885–1965*. The first monograph of the artist was published in 2016 by Sansom & Company, written by Guy Peploe.

Opposite: Pat Douthwaite, c.1980

Right: *Pat Douthwaite* by Guy Peploe, Sansom & Company, 2016

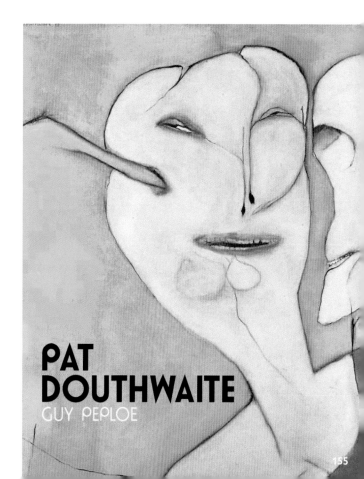

PAT DOUTHWAITE
GUY PEPLOE

155

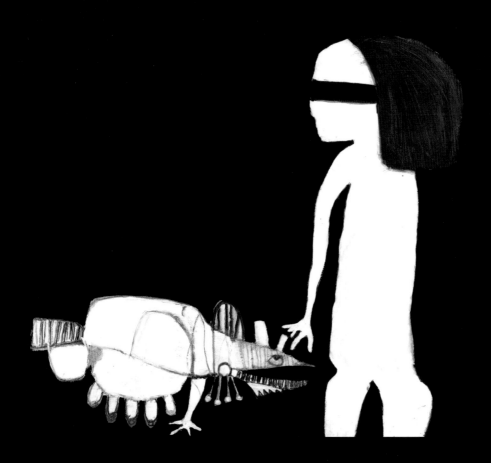

Above: Pat Douthwaite, Blindfold, 1965, oil on board, 80 x 95 cms. Acquired from The Scottish Gallery by the Scottish National Gallery of Modern Art, Edinburgh, 2013

Douthwaite's drawings are often done in series, swift workings of an idea which will develop in the making. Her anthropomorphism is sometimes poignant, often hilarious and reflects both her deep sympathy for the animal world and unflinching eye for human character and foible.

Opposite: Cat.59, Pat Douthwaite, Stripper Cockerel, 1990, charcoal & pastel, 82 x 58 cms, Exhibited: *Pat Douthwaite – Memorial Exhibition*, The Scottish Gallery, Edinburgh, 2006, cat.28; *The Outsider*, The Scottish Gallery, Edinburgh, 2016, cat. 29

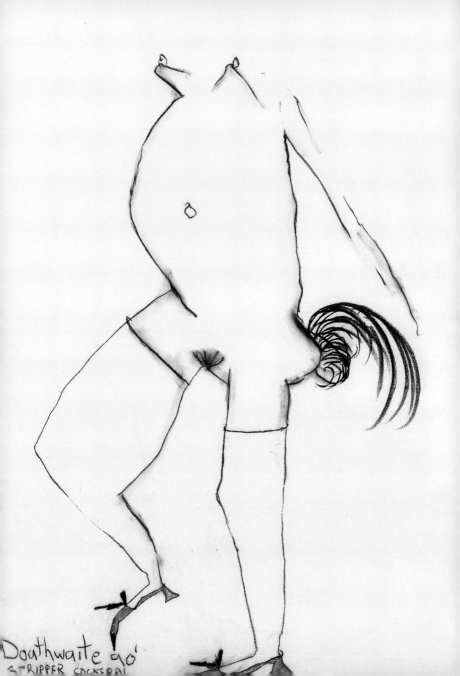

Douthwaite 90'
STRIPPER COCKTAIL

Cat.60, Pat Douthwaite, The Cloak (1974–75), oil on canvas, 142.5 x 142 cms.
Exhibited: *The Outsider*, The Scottish Gallery, Edinburgh, 2016, ex cat

*The Cloak*, as with so many of Douthwaite's compositions, satisfies both psychological and decorative demands. The patterned cloak (she has a magpie and unerring eye for design) and pitch black background lend visual drama, while the cloaked figure remains enigmatic: is she dancer, Mata Hari or an Egyptian goddess? The artist's great contribution is her consistent depiction on the single, female figure: her American Bandits, Goddesses, Amy Johnson, Mary Queen of Scots and so on are, in one sense are all self-portraiture.

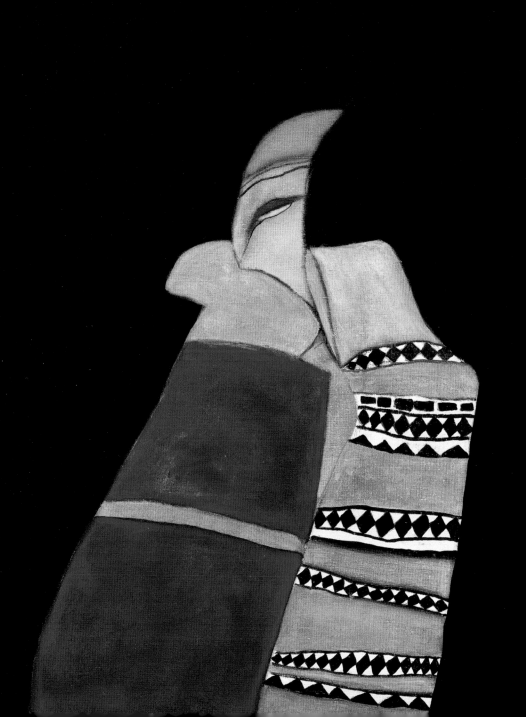

## BARBARA RAE
### CBE, RA, RSA, RGI, RSW (b.1943)

Barbara Rae was born in 1943 in Falkirk and attended Edinburgh College of Art for her Diploma and post-Dip studies. She taught at The Glasgow School of Art from 1975 until 1996. She had the first of twelve one-person shows with The Scottish Gallery in 1979, the last mounted to launch the publication of the Lund Humphries monograph *Barbara Rae* in 2008. While we no longer represent her we always have her work available in The Gallery.

Barbara Rae consistently demonstrates an ability to lend the landscape a tonal truth which recreates the experience of place. She has travelled widely to find her subject but will eschew a literal meaning and will often choose an unconventional viewpoint or include enigmatic or derelict components.

In *Derelict Boat at Dornie* her territory is still landscape and a dark horizon is more than suggested, but the interior of the boat, its prow set to the wave of its memory, its wooden ribs and planks catching the colours of the fading day, make a flattened abstract pattern which has become the equivalent of the experience of seeing rather than its result.

Cat.61, Barbara Rae, Derelict Boat at Dornie, 1989, mixed media and collage on canvas, 81 x 110 cms.
Exhibited: *Landmarks and Docklands*, The Scottish Gallery, London. Provenance: Private collection, Alloa

Cat.62, Barbara Rae, *Lanjaron Field*, 1989, mixed media on board, 81.5 x 109 cms.
Exhibited: *The Scottish Gallery At Arco 90*, International Contemporary Art Fair, Madrid, January 1990;
*Modern Masters IV*, The Scottish Gallery, Edinburgh, February 2015, cat.36. Provenance: Private collection, Edinburgh

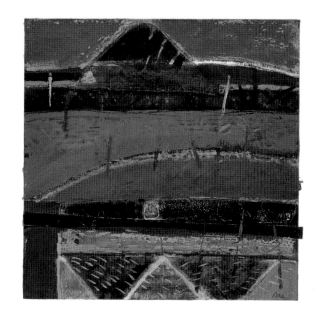

Cat.63, Barbara Rae, Skye Fence, 1984, mixed media on board, 19.5 x 20 cms

## VICTORIA CROWE
### OBE, DHC, FRSE, MA(RCA), RSA, RSW (b.1945)

Victoria Crowe has been described as 'one of the most vital and original figurative painters currently at work in Scotland' with works in global public and private collections, including the National Portrait Gallery, London; National Galleries of Scotland; the Royal Academy, London; and Frederiksborg Castle, Denmark. Over the last 40 years she has established herself as a painter whose work is instantly recognisable and while the full range of her painting covers landscape, still lifes, portraits, self-portraits and interiors, much of her work defies such precise categorisation.

Victoria studied at Kingston School of Art (1961–65) and at the Royal College of Art, London (1965–68). For 30 years she worked as a part-time lecturer in the School of Drawing and Painting at Edinburgh College of Art, while developing her own artistic practice. Her first one person exhibition, after leaving the Royal College of Art, was in London and she has subsequently gone on to have over 50 solo shows worldwide.

Victoria is a member of the Royal Scottish Academy (RSA) and the Royal Scottish Society of Painters in Watercolours (RSW). She has exhibited nationally and internationally and undertaken many important portrait commissions, including RD Laing, Peter Higgs and Jocelyn Bell Burnell. In 2018, the Scottish National Portrait Gallery is holding a retrospective exhibition of Crowe's portrait work, which will coincide with an Edinburgh Festival Exhibition of new paintings at The Scottish Gallery.

Victoria Crowe in her studio. Photo: Kenneth Gray

Above: Cat.64, Numinous Tree, 2010, oil on panel, 71 x 76 cms. Exhibited: *Victoria Crowe – Reflection*, The Scottish Gallery, Edinburgh, 2010, cat.16. Provenance: Private Collection, London

Opposite: Cat.65, Studio Interior with Mask, c.2009, oil on linen, 71 x76 cms

## KATE DOWNIE
RSA, PPSSA (b.1958)

Born in North Carolina, Kate Downie studied at Grays School of Art in Aberdeen before travel and residencies took her to the United States, England, Amsterdam and Paris. Downie is one of the most subtle and persuasive colourists of her generation and she will only add to her palette from real experience. This gives her work a truth and authority, a right to transport us to the unfamiliar or provide an urgent reminder of where we have also been. Kate's constant search for new challenges and inspirations has seen her set up studios in such diverse places as a brewery, an oil rig, and an abandoned Hydroponicum.

Public Collections include:

Aberdeen Art Gallery
Aberdeen Asset Management
Aberdeen University
Borders General Hospital
Grampian Regional Council
Adam & Co, Merchant Bank
Allied Breweries
Art in Healthcare, Scotland
Cleveland Art Gallery,
Middlesbrough
City of Edinburgh Council
Edinburgh City Arts Centre
Glasgow Gallery of Modern Art
Gracefield Museums and
Galleries, Dumfries
Gray's School of Art, Aberdeen

HM the Queen
Kelvingrove Art Gallery, Glasgow
Kirkcaldy Art Gallery and Museum
Museum of London
New Hall Art Collection,
Cambridge
Rietveld Kunst Academie,
Amsterdam
Robert Gordon University,
Aberdeen
Royal Bank of Scotland
Royal Scottish Academy,
Edinburgh
Scottish Arts Council
The University of Edinburgh

Kate Downie in her studio, January 2015.
Photo: Michael Wolchover

Tokyo (The Hand), 2017, oil on canvas, 110 x 200 cms.
Exhibited: *The Anatomy of Haste*, The Scottish Gallery, Edinburgh, 2017

/ SIX /

# Contemporaries

MATTHEW DRAPER – AMONGST THE CLOUDS

JOHN BROWN Centro Habana

HENRY KONDRACKI Three Cities

The Romanticism, Folklore and Fantasy of Michael McVeigh

DUNCAN SHANKS WORKS ON PAPER 1957-2013

DAVID CASS YEARS OF DUST AND DRY

GEOFF UGLOW THE ROSE GARDEN VOL 1 MMXVI

KATE DOWNIE ESTUARY

DAVID COOK SAVAGE TRANQUILLITY

Elizabeth Blackadder DECADES

LIFE STUDIES

PHILIP BRAHAM KEEPING TIME

DAVID EUSTACE SELECTED WORKS

PAUL REID MYTH MAKING

VICTORIA CROWE Light on the Landscape

wnie The Coast Road Diaries 2007 to 2009

CALUM McCLURE NOCTURNES & BOTANICS

FLORA DEPICTA

# Contemporaries

In art world parlance if you are described as contemporary you are alive; if you are modern you will have passed! For The Scottish Gallery the most important aspect of our programme is the exhibition of new work and in particular one person shows. These become milestones in an artist's career, opportunities to clear the studio and head space, to explore one or more themes and generate sufficient sales to sustain life for the next year or two. Inevitably the work illustrated in this section looks forward to our unfolding exhibition programme and perhaps needs less commentary.

Our upper gallery for 175th anniversary month is unapologetically dedicated to our senior landscape painter Duncan Shanks (in his eightieth year), just as our chief contribution to the Edinburgh Festival has always been a new-work, one-person show each August, this year provided by Kate Downie. 175 seems like an extraordinary span of time and indeed it is, but there are many instances of long, fruitful relationships with artists which put this in context. Dr James Morrison has shown here for fifty-nine years and counting; Lord Haig showed consistently from 1945 until his triumphant ninetieth birthday exhibition in 2006. Houston, Blackadder, Michie and many more passed forty years of representation. Who can say that from our current crop of young painters some will still be showing beyond our 225th anniversary? The commitment to an exhibition of new work every two or three years from both artist and gallery describes the raison d'etre and business plan for The Scottish Gallery and the ideal career path for the artist. The Scottish Gallery has never tried to lead taste, but has often done so; Alison Watt's first solo exhibition was with us in 1990, as was S.J. Peploe's in 1903 and Calum McClure in 2011. We try to maintain a current programme which embraces many media, a philosophy not limited to belle peinture but neither denying the importance of the concept of beauty, and above all to take creative risk in partnership with the talented individuals who plenish our programme.

For The Scottish Gallery the most important aspect of our programme is the exhibition of new work and in particular one person shows. These become milestones in an artist's career, opportunities to clear the studio and head space, to explore one or more themes and generate sufficient sales to sustain life for the next year or two.

Previous: Geoff Uglow, Solstice MMXVI, 2017, oil on board, 200 x 210 cms (detail). Exhibited: *The Rose Garden, Volume 1*, The Scottish Gallery, Edinburgh, 2017, cat. 22

Left: Selection of contemporary catalogues, 2009–2017

# HUGH BUCHANAN (b.1958)

Hugh Buchanan was born in Edinburgh in 1958. The city instilled in him a love of architecture which he developed as a student of Drawing and Painting at Edinburgh College of Art. The artist's chosen medium is watercolour, of which he has become a master. His palette, so evocative of the nuance of time and place and his control of tone and line are impeccable allowing him ample means to explore his subject.

After graduating in 1981 he worked on commissions for the National Trust and in 1987 was invited by the Prince of Wales to paint a series of interiors of Balmoral, subsequently completing a further sequence at Highgrove in 1994. In 1988 he was commissioned by the House of Commons to paint four interiors of the Palace of Westminster. In 1998 five works by Hugh Buchanan were included in the exhibition Princes as Patrons: The Art Collections of the Princes of Wales from the Renaissance to the Present Day shown at the National Museum and Gallery, Cardiff. In 2002 he was commissioned by the House of Lords to paint the lying in state of the Queen Mother at the Palace of Westminster. In 2005 his paintings featured in Watercolours and Drawings from the Collection of Queen Elizabeth the Queen Mother, at the Palace of Holyroodhouse, Edinburgh and Queen's Gallery, London. In 2013 he was invited by the National Library of Scotland to paint a series of compositions of The John Murray Archive which were exhibited at the National Library in 2015. His painting of Patrick Leigh Fermor's passports was presented to the National Library in 2016.

His most recent exhibition New Town, his fourth with The Scottish Gallery, is to be held in The Gallery in June 2017. The exhibition coincides with the 250th anniversary of Edinburgh's New Town.

Hugh Buchanan in his
East Lothian studio, 2017.
Photo: Stephen Dunn

St Stephens Reflection, watercolour, 56 x 38 cms. Exhibited: *New Town*, The Scottish Gallery, Edinburgh, 2017, cat. 34

## DAVID CASS
## ARWS (b.1988)

David Cass was born in Edinburgh, and brought up
in the Scottish Borders. He graduated with First Class
Honours from Edinburgh College of Art in 2010,
receiving the Royal Scottish Academy's John Kinross
Scholarship to Florence. The RSA now holds six of
his artworks in their permanent collection.

Recently elected an associate member of the
Royal Watercolour Society, David Cass is difficult to
pigeon-hole as he works across such a wide variety of
media. He's had four painting-based solo exhibitions
with The Gallery since graduating. At the age of just 22
Cass constructed his inaugural show – *Unearthed* which
was followed by the more conceptual *Years of Dust and Dry*
in 2013, an exhibition describing Florence's Great Flood
of 1966: *Tonight Rain, Tomorrow Mud* in 2015. His most
recent exhibition, *Pelada* was held in January 2017 and
captured the unseen beauty of Venice.

Cass has taken a series of research trips onto mainland Europe
over the last few months, preparing new painted works and
collaborating with environmentally focused arts organisations.
One recent project of note is his work inspired by the devastating
floods that swept Florence in 1966. In his own words:

'Inspired by photographic documentation – from press, postcards,
residents' photographs – and from imagination, I've painted scenes
with antique paints, on antique papers, card and wood. I began
creating these artworks in late in 2013: 47 years after the flood which
claimed over 100 lives in and around the city and destroyed hundreds
of thousands of works of art and precious documents. I first visited
Florence in late 2010, on a Royal Scottish Academy scholarship.
I've returned several times since 2010, and my artistic response to
the city has gradually developed.'

Right: A Selection of work from David's
exhibition *Pelada*, January 2017

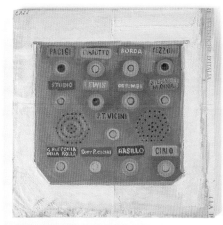

## DAVID EUSTACE (b.1961)

In 2015, The Gallery hosted a survey exhibition on the work of David Eustace. This was our first solo photography exhibition and also the first time that David Eustace's work was available to the public for sale.

David Eustace is widely regarded as a photographer's photographer. Living between Edinburgh and New York, he has worked for many major magazines and his list of sitters reads like a Who's Who in the world of art, cinema, music and design; Tracey Emin to Sir Peter Blake, Sophia Loren to James Earl Jones, Radiohead to Sir Paul McCartney, Lord Norman Foster to Milton Glaser. But his work is not restricted to portraiture; he also works in fashion, landscape, and documentary projects.

Eustace's work is held in both public and private collections worldwide, including Deutsche Bank, The National Portrait Gallery, London, and The Glasgow Museum of Modern Art.

In 2011, he was awarded an Honorary Doctor of Arts from Edinburgh Napier University, where he now serves as Chancellor.

**Left: David Eustace, 2015.**
**Photo: Scott Douglas**

Cat.66, Highland Heart Portfolio (Plate No. 13),
Detail of gravestone, Western Highlands, 2012,
edition of 15, archival pigment print, 81 x 106 cms

'I began this portfolio in 2012 with the support of American clothing giant Anthropologie. Created in the Western Highlands and Hebridean Islands of Scotland, 42 large scale works from this ongoing portfolio were exhibited in New York City in 2013, sponsored by The Scottish Government. I'm not comfortable with the term 'capture' when it comes to describe how I make my images, as this suggests a wish to possess, restrict or even imprison something, and the spirit of this land belongs to no man. My hope is that these images offer a window on a moment, a split second when this land smiled at me and I felt humbled.' — David Eustace, 2015

Cat.67, David Eustace, John Byrne in Yellow Tweed Suit,
Glasgow, 2011, edition of 25, archival pigment print,
133 x 110 cms. Public Collection, Scottish National Portrait
Gallery, Edinburgh

David Eustace is currently working towards a series of images
entitled *Friends and Artists (The Simple Portrait)* which will be
held at The Scottish Gallery in 2018. The project in David's own
words features 'folk who inspire me or interest me, who make
me question or perhaps offer answers'. David's portrait of
John Byrne (opposite) was acquired by the Scottish National
Portrait Gallery in 2011.

# LACHLAN GOUDIE
## ROI (b.1976)

Lachlan Goudie was born in Glasgow and now lives and works in London as an artist, writer, and broadcaster. He is the son of the figurative painter Alexander Goudie. He exhibits regularly in London and New York and will be holding his first solo show at The Scottish Gallery in 2018.

After studying English Literature at Cambridge University, Lachlan was awarded the prestigious Levy-Plumb scholarship, a yearlong painting residency at Christ's College. In 1999 he was awarded the R.S.P. Prize for painting at the Royal Glasgow Institute of Fine Arts and in 2001 the Norman MacFarlane prize at the Royal Scottish Academy. Lachlan graduated in June 2004 from Camberwell College of Arts with a degree in Fine Art and Painting. In 2011 he was a prize winner at the annual exhibition of The Royal Institute of Painters in Oil Colour, he has been a full member of The ROI since 2013.

The scope of Lachlan's work is broad, evolving from a figurative tradition of Scottish painting to incorporate still life and landscape. He is often inspired from his travels and draws on the works of great masters and Matisse, Sargent, Manet and Velazquez.

Lachlan broadcasts regularly on the BBC radio programme, *From our own Correspondent* and has written and presented a documentary for BBC4 about the history of witches in art. He most recently hosted a BBC4 broadcast *The Story of Scottish Art*, a television series mapping the last 5000 years of Scottish Art history.

'It's a great pleasure for me to exhibit at The Scottish Gallery, where my father had many of his most distinguished exhibitions. I'm looking forward to the opportunity of showing a range of work especially created for the gallery along with a selection of paintings from recent years.'

— Lachlan Goudie, 2017

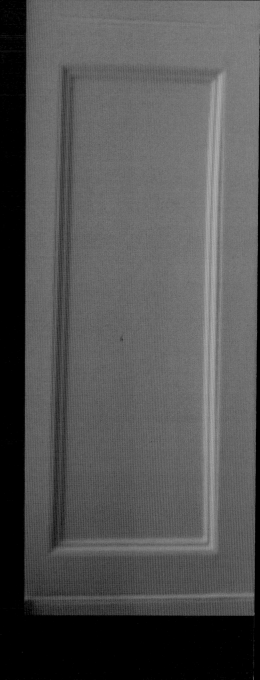

# DERRICK GUILD
## RSA (b.1963)

Born in 1963 in Perth, Derrick Guild has been the recipient of many awards for his unique work. He graduated from Duncan of Jordanstone College of Art & Design in the late 80's and Guild's paintings and objects reference European still life of the 15th to 19th centuries. From 1983–1987, he attended Duncan of Jordanstone College of Art and Design, in Dundee, Scotland, where he received a First Class Honours BA in Fine Art, and Postgraduate Diploma, Highly Commended. The drama, allegory and naturalism inherent in this period of painting speak to Guild of ever-present dilemmas in the human condition. His works are classical, formal and at the same time contemporary in their sense of dislocation and ambiguity.

'I find the general degradation of old botanical and animal paintings particularly interesting. It is almost as if nature is forcing its unruly mark back onto what is often a scientifically correct and for me quite soulless rendering of a flower. The foxed and stained illusionistic paper that I paint has become a theatre, or space that my flowers and animals can inhabit. I was lucky enough to spend two years on Ascension Island in the South Atlantic where I had first-hand experience of tropical and sub-tropical plants. What really struck me about these wonderful flowers was their powerful, sticky and relentless fecundity. The less than pure paper that I render in paint is a manifestation of that fecundity.' — Derrick Guild, 2016

Right: Follower, 2016 (detail)

Opposite: Cast (Brecht's Journal), 2016/2017, acrylic on linen, 142 x 112 cms. Exhibited: *Brecht's Journal*, The Scottish Gallery, Edinburgh, 2017

187

## ANGIE LEWIN
### RWS, RE (b.1963)

Angie Lewin was born in Cheshire and studied BA(Hons) Fine Art Printmaking at Central St. Martins College of Art and Design between 1983 and 1986, followed by a year's part-time postgraduate printmaking at Camberwell School of Arts and Crafts. After working in London as an illustrator she studied horticulture and then subsequently moved to Norfolk, which prompted a return to printmaking. Angie now mainly lives and works in Scotland.

Inspired by both the clifftops and saltmarshes of the North Norfolk coast and the Scottish Highlands, she depicts these contrasting environments and their native flora in wood engraving, linocut, silkscreen, lithograph and collage. These landscapes are often glimpsed through intricately detailed plantforms. Attracted to the relationships between plant communities on an intimate level, even the fine lines of insect eggs on a flower bud are observed in her work. Still lives often incorporate seedpods, grasses, flints and dried seaweed collected on walking and sketching trips. A Wedgwood cup designed by Ravilious, may contain feathers and seed heads.

In 2010 Merrell published the monograph *Angie Lewin – Plants and Places*. As well as designing fabrics and stationery for St Jude's, which Angie runs with her husband Simon, she has completed commissions for Penguin, Faber, Conran Octopus, Merrell and Picador and has also designed fabrics for Liberty.

In 2006 Angie was elected to The Royal Society of Painter Printmakers and in 2008 to The Society of Wood Engravers. In 2010 she was elected to The Art Workers Guild and in 2016 she was elected to The Royal Watercolour Society.

Public collections include:
Victoria & Albert Museum, London
The Ashmolean Museum, Oxford
The London Institute
The University of Aberystwyth
Art for Hospitals and Hospices Collection

Angie in her Edinburgh Studio, 2014

The Blue Platter, 2015, watercolour, 55 x 77 cms.
Exhibited: *A Natural Selection*, The Scottish Gallery, Edinburgh, 2015, cat. 12. Sold by The Gallery, 2015

## CALUM MCCLURE (b.1987)

Calum McClure was born in 1987 and graduated in Drawing and Painting from Edinburgh College of Art in 2010. McClure's drawings, prints and paintings depict country estates, cemeteries, national parks and botanical gardens – places created for man's solace and pleasure. He thinks about these places as a modern Arcadia; into which people can escape for a few hours every week. Through a varied use of paint McClure explores the complexity of images taken from nature that at first look simple. The motif of reflection has become important in his work, challenging the viewer to think about what has been painted and the tactile nature of the painting process. Recent work has taken inspiration from various source images, including film stills, photographs from train windows and other photographs taken whilst walking. He is currently working on ideas and themes including: nocturne, botanic gardens, the idea of an 'in-between image', and more generally light and its reflective qualities.

He was the winner of the inaugural Jolomo Painting Award in 2011 and was an invited artist at the Annual Exhibition at the Royal Academy in London in 2012. Recently he has been included in an exhibition of prints at the Royal Academy; had work in the major Scottish art societies' annual exhibitions; exhibited at the RA Summer Exhibition 2016 and won a prize at the W Gordon Smith Award for painting in 2016. His next solo exhibition will be in October 2018, his third with The Scottish Gallery.

Cat.68, American Football Dream, Stadtpark, Hamburg, 2014, oil on canvas, 100 x 110 cms

## BARRY MCGLASHAN (b.1974)

Barry McGlashan has talent to burn; he draws
with eloquence, has a distinctive, bright palette
which feeds into the ethereal world he can
invent, and his compositions are consistently
satisfying. But these gifts would be of so much less
interest if he had nothing to say. His schooling in
Aberdeen and the influence of Alexander Fraser
encouraged him to become a storyteller, but
with a magical realist slant. He creates enigmatic
narratives, where his human participants are often
dwarfed by an heroic landscape or he steps into a
medieval world created (in our imagination) by a
Renaissance master.

Right: *The Sunken Dream*
exhibition catalogue, June 2014

Opposite: Barry McGlashan
in his studio, January 2017

## PAUL REID (b.1975)

I first became aware of Paul Reid's paintings when I was a lecturer at Duncan of Jordanstone College of Art in the mid-nineties. As part of the first year course schedule students were asked to make a self-portrait. I remember being very taken with the small head and shoulders self-portrait that Paul produced. The painting had something of the warmth of colouring of Van Dyck and the cool gaze of Velázquez. It showed a precocious talent with serious intent that said to me that this was someone to watch.

In the subsequent four years Paul devoured Max Doerner's *The Materials of the Artist and their Use in Painting*. He learned to grind pigments and make a paint that had the desired consistency for his works. At the same time Paul also immersed himself in studying Rubens, Van Dyck, Titian and Velázquez, the artists whose techniques he sought to emulate. Paul was painting wonderfully assured realist still lifes and thoroughly engaging portraits of family and friends. The still life works and portraits were powerfully realistic with an ease of handling that showed his deep understanding of the language of the Masters he was studying. It was while studying Rubens that Paul became interested in mythological based works. Through studying the titles and names referred to by Rubens he became aware that they referred to Greek myths. In a sense Paul was led to classical mythology by the process of painting itself. Paul began studying Ovid's Metamorphoses which opened up a vast subject where he could expand, channel and challenge his formidable powers of realistic painting, over the next 15 years. Paul's first classically inspired work was a large painting *The Death of Actaeon* painted in his fourth year. This was a very significant transitional point for Paul: it was where his portraiture, life room studies and

still life knowledge were all pulled together into one large successful composition. It was intriguing at the time to leave his studio and see the faces of the characters of his paintings wandering the art school corridors.

Paul's subsequent ongoing body of mythologically inspired paintings have worked so well because of his powers to instil a potent sense of reality. It is not an arcane or unreachable reality but something timeless and tangible.

— Derick Guild, RSA, quoted from *Mythologies* exhibition catalogue, August 2013

**Opposite: Cat.69, Philoctetes, 2016, oil on canvas, 75 x 100 cms**

'Philoctetes was one of the Greek commanders who set off to invade the city of Troy with Agamemnon, Achilles, Odysseus etc. He was the owner of the famous 'Bow of Hercules' which the great hero had given him as he died. The bow and poisoned arrows never missed their target.

On the journey towards Troy the fleet stopped off at Tenedos to sacrifice to the God Apollo. Unfortunately, Philoctetes was bitten on the ankle by a poisonous snake and the wound festered and would not heal. The Greeks were forced to leave Philoctetes on the Island of Lemnos as they could no longer suffer his constant anguished cries of pain.

Philoctetes survived alone on the island with the help of his bow and arrows. After 10 years, the Greeks were forced to return to Lemnos in order to persuade Philoctetes to journey with them to Troy after a prophet foretold that they could not take the city without the Bow of Hercules.

Troy was eventually taken with the help of Philoctetes who shot the Trojan prince Paris with a poisonous arrow.' — Paul Reid

## GEOFF UGLOW (b.1978)

Geoff Uglow was born and raised in Cornwall, but trained at the Glasgow School of Art, where he won numerous awards, including the John Cunningham Award and the McKendrick Scholarship. Following his degree he was awarded the Sainsbury Scholarship to study at the British School of Rome, where he studied for two years, before returning to Cornwall, where he now lives and works.

Working in carefully layered paint, in a manner that has become almost sculptural, Uglow's technique is inspired in equal measure by Roman frescoes and Modernist painting. Taking the tradition of landscape painting and its relation to Romantic poetry as his subject, Uglow explores the notion of history and its meaning in the present. For his most recent works Geoff Uglow has found inspiration in his rose garden, which he has cultivated from seed. Geoff has had five solo exhibitions with The Scottish Gallery.

For the moment the rose is special. It encapsulates everything I need in a subject. It is beautiful but also violent. It is lovely, seductive and tragic. It has a life. It is growing and changing.'

— Geoff Uglow, 2017

Cat.70, 12–10–16, oil on board, 60 x 70 cms.
Exhibited: *The Rose Garden Volume 1*, The Scottish Gallery, Edinburgh, 2017, cat.18

# SEVEN

# The Print Department

# Prints at The Scottish Gallery
## — Iain A. Barnet

An abiding memory of my first few days at The Scottish Gallery is being introduced to the print department by Ronnie Miller (the framing department manager for 49 years). Solander box after solander box was taken out to show me – their heavy weight, the texture of their binding, the slap of their lids on the counter – then revealed, leafed between acid-free tissue and mounted on acid-free board, were original etchings by Rembrandt, landscape capriccios from Paul Sandby, miniature etchings by John Clerk of Eldin, velvety mezzotints after portraits by Henry Raeburn, dark, iconic landscapes from D.Y. Cameron, some etched *joie de vivre* from Anthony Gross, or charmingly 'primitive' seventeenth-century maps by Johannes Blaeu. In adjacent print cabinets were found more recent, larger works – lithographs by Colquhoun and MacBryde, etchings from Julian Trevelyan and John Piper, screenprints by Patrick Heron and Robyn Denny, and others by David Hockney, Eduardo Paolozzi, Norman Ackroyd, Elisabeth Frink and a host of contemporary Scottish printmakers. Clearly, the print department of 1987 represented The Gallery at its most eclectic!

**CHARLES HODGE MACKIE
RSA, RSW (1862–1920)**

Cat.71, Children Playing on a Terraza, Venice, coloured woodblock print, 42 x 58 cms

Previous: Wilhelmina Barns-Graham, Orange & Red on Pink (detail), 1960–91, screenprint, 76.3 x 48.5 cms, edition of 70 (Cat.80)

The Scottish Gallery has had a long and fruitful relationship with printmaking, as dealers, exhibitors and at times, publishers. In the 1890s, Aitken Dott & Sons published a number of steel engravings after popular paintings such as *The Meeting of Burns and Scott* by Charles Martin Hardie. At the same time, and for many years to come, the company held large stocks of antiquarian prints – etchings by Albrecht Dürer, engravings from *Le Vedute di Roma* by Piranesi, eighteenth-century caricatures from George Cruikshank, etchings of Paris by Charles Méryon and William Daniell's 1820s aquatints from *A Voyage Round Great Britain*, among many, many others. Alongside works from the past, the print department of 1900 was well stocked with contemporary artists, including etching pioneers such as American James Abbott McNeill Whistler, the Swede Anders Zorn, Scotsman William Strang and Frenchman Alphonse Legros.

**D.Y. CAMERON
RA (1865–1945)**

Cat.72, Loch Ard, 1924,
etching, 8.5 × 20 cms

**JAMES MCBEY
(1883–1959)**

Cat.73, September Sunset,
Venice, 1924, etching,
22 × 45 cms,
edition of 50

**FRANCES WALKER**

Cat.74, Grytviken,
South Georgia, 2010,
etching and aquatint,
22.5 × 55 cms,
edition of 12

Cat.75, Above: Alison Watt, Narcissus, 1997, screenprint, 63 x 51 cms, edition of 100

Opposite: Cat.76, John Byrne, Girl with Monkey, 1972, coloured etching, 35 x 25 cms, edition of 12

*Girl with Monkey* was the first print John Byrne ever made, commissioned by Glasgow Print Studio shortly after its opening in 1972. The etching is signed 'Patrick', a persona Byrne first adopted in 1967. Having been greatly interested in the work of primitive painters for a number of years, Byrne sent some of his own paintings to the Portal Gallery in London with a letter stating that they had been created by his father, Patrick, who had received no formal art training.

'The monkey refers to the one he was promised he would be given by an uncle on his return from Burma in 1945. No monkey was forthcoming.' — Robert Hewison, *John Byrne: Art and Life*, Lund Humphries, 2011, p.39

The Edwardian era through to the Second World War saw a great vogue for the freedom of line and monochrome textures of etchings, which, with wide-margined mounts and narrow black frames, graced many a fashionable interior of the period. Many of the finest exponents of etching were Scots (to such an extent that etching was regarded almost as a national art form), epitomised by the avidly collected work of Muirhead Bone, James McBey, D.Y. Cameron and E.S. Lumsden, all of whom were exhibited by The Gallery. Despite this local pre-eminence, non-Scots continued to be stocked – Frank Brangwyn, G.L. Brockhurst, Edmund Blampied, Robert Austin and Laura Knight, to name but a few. Gallery records show that its publication of a series of original etchings by Joseph Gray in the late twenties proved highly successful, with prints selling rapidly to collectors in New York, Philadelphia, Chicago and London.

Concurrent with the interwar boom in etching was a growing appreciation for woodblock printing, inspired by the Japanese and filtered through French post-impressionism. In 1911 The Gallery had shown woodblock prints by Hokusai and Utamaro, and artists such as Charles Hodge Mackie and Mabel Royds, who were inspired by such masters, later showed with The Gallery.

With post-war austerity, many artists and dealers saw printmaking as a more affordable way of bringing original contemporary art to a wider audience. In the 1940s and 50s, this idea in part sparked a renewed interest in the painterly qualities of lithography, and encouraged Edinburgh-based printer Harley Brothers to commission a large series of lithographs from contemporary painters. A number of Scottish Gallery artists were invited to participate, with Anne Redpath, Robin Philipson, Earl

Above: Cat.77, Colquhoun, Cornish Woman with Goat, 1948, lithograph, 37.5 x 27.5 cms, edition of 8. Exhibited: *The Golden Years*, The Scottish Gallery, Edinburgh, 2014, cat. 10. Provenance: Private collection, Dumfries & Galloway. Illustrated: *The Last Bohemians* by Roger Bristow, 2010, illustrated [017] p.208

Opposite: Cat.78, Robert MacBryde, Still Life II, c.1960, lithograph, 64 x 52 cms. Exhibited: Barbizon Gallery, Glasgow, 1996; *The Golden Years*, The Scottish Gallery, Edinburgh, 2014, cat. 31. Provenance: Private collection, Dumfries & Galloway. Illustrated: *The Last Bohemians by Roger Bristow*, 2010, illustrated [024] p.208

Haig, William and David McClure, among others, producing memorable 'Edinburgh School' images.

The 1960s and 70s saw the opening up of print workshops in all of Scotland's major cities, providing the facilities, equipment and expertise to allow many more artists to experiment with printmaking. Numerous Scottish Gallery painters took up this opportunity – Wilhelmina Barns-Graham, John Houston, Barbara Rae, Elizabeth Blackadder, John Bellany, Victoria Crowe, John Byrne – and greatly expanded their oeuvres by doing so. In the early 1980s The Gallery returned to publishing, with a series of original lithographs – a typically emotive sunset from John Houston and some mystic symbols from Alan Davie, for example – and in the 1990s was joint publisher of The Sutherland Suite, a series of groundbreaking etchings from Barbara Rae.

Print highlights I recall from my fifteen years with The Gallery include a major show of monotypes and screenprints from the mercurial Bruce McLean, a moving collection of etchings by Ian Fleming, the first joint exhibition of prints by John Houston and Elizabeth Blackadder, engraved portraits of seventeenth-century nobility by Robert Nanteuil, the poised minimalism of master printmaker Philip Reeves and a show from Glasgow Print Studio that included works from the then New Glasgow Boys, Steven Campbell, Stephen Conroy, Peter Howson and Adrian Wiszniewski.

With The Gallery's move from 94 George Street to their current premises, the print department closed. Yet The Scottish Gallery continues to exhibit printmaking at its best, perhaps with a return to the more international outlook of earlier days, evidenced by recent shows of William Wilson, Picasso and the École de Paris.

— Iain A. Barnet is a former Director of The Scottish Gallery where he worked from 1987 to 2001.

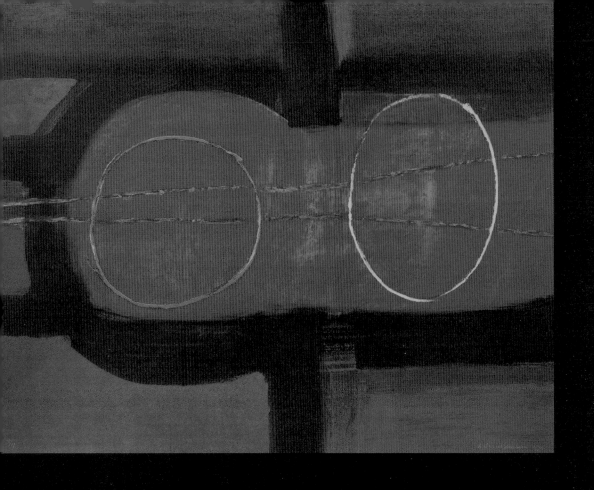

Above: Cat.79, Wilhelmina Barns-Graham, Two Circles on Purple, 1992, lithograph, 60 x 75.5 cms, edition of 70

Opposite: Cat.80, Wilhelmina Barns-Graham, Orange & Red on Pink, 1960–91, screenprint, 76.3 x 48.5 cms, edition of 70

## JOHN BELLANY
### CBE, RA (1942–2013)

John Bellany was born in Port Seton, a fishing village on the Forth estuary and his spiritual home. The symbolism of the sea, the live catch, the predatory gull, the bereaved-eye of the fisher-folk for whom the sea is both endless bounty and a harsh mistress recur in his work, particularly up until his liver transplantation in 1985. Bellany's nervous line and chiaroscuro work brilliantly in intaglio print making where his heroes Rembrandt and Goya were also preeminent. His family, Presbyterian upbringing, the freedom of the public-house and the company of poets and artists as well as a frank exploration of his own demons provide fecund material in a series of small edition etchings, drypoints and mezzotints which rank as some of his most successful artworks. John Bellany first showed with The Gallery in 1986. Further exhibitions have been held in 2005 and 2013.

Cat.81, John Bellany, Self Portrait in Hospital II, 1988, etching, 45 x 40 cms, edition of 20

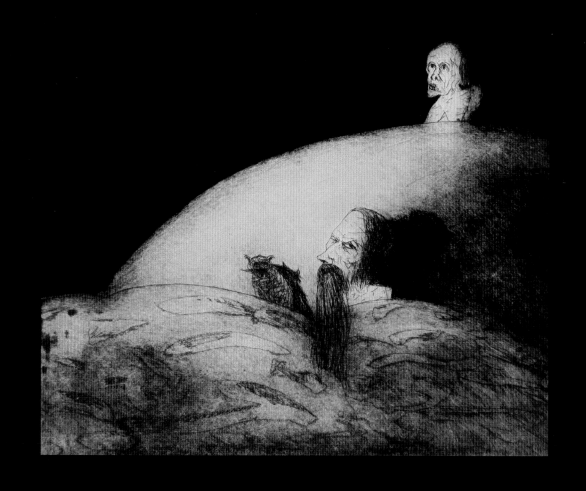

Cat.82, John Bellany, Death Knell, 1972, etching, 47 x 47 cms, edition of 75

Above: Cat.83, Elizabeth Blackadder, Wild Flowers, 2013, screenprint, 89.5 x 72.5 cms, edition of 75

Opposite: Cat.84, Barbara Rae, Sierra, 2006, screenprint, 115 x 80 cms, edition of 30

Cat.85, Victoria Crowe, Italian Offerings, c.1995, lithograph, 57 x 70.5 cms, edition of 20

Cat.86, Victoria Crowe, Against the Light, Warmer Change, 2015/2016, monoprint, 57 x 67 cms.
Exhibited: *Light on the Landscape*, The Scottish Gallery, Edinbugrh, 2016, cat.34

Cat.87, Angie Lewin, Cromarty Bowl, 2014, lithograph, 19 x 20.5 cms, edition of 10

Cat.88, Angie Lewin, Honesty Blue, 2015, screenprint, 37 x 58 cms, edition of 150

Adam Buick, Large Moon Jar, 2016, Pembrokeshire, Wales, H40 x W33 cms

/ EIGHT /

# The World of Objects

# The World of Objects

The World of Objects is an outstanding area of The Gallery, making the experience of coming through our door an odyssey of discovery. Our objects form part of a comprehensive programme of innovative and diverse monthly exhibitions, covering a wide range of disciplines, such as ceramics, glass, jewellery, metalwork, sculpture and textiles. Our reputation has been hard won over decades, and we champion some of the most remarkable work in each field, from Scotland, the UK and the rest of the world. We maintain a careful balance of emerging, established and senior talents, who sit side by side, often with strong, opposing and contrasting practices, from traditional craft to more narrative and conceptual work. Our exhibitions are all of museum standard; it is important to The Gallery that we make accessible to our audience beautifully made, traditional work alongside the extraordinary and surprising. The Scottish Gallery belongs to a community of artists and collectors who are all interconnected and we value above all our relationships with our artists and our clients who respond to their work.

When Henry Rothschild invited Lucie Rie and Hans Coper to take part in one of his seminal survey shows in the late 1970s, he set a benchmark for quality in the field of ceramics. Jennifer Lee held her first solo exhibition at The Gallery and Edmund de Waal, Julian Stair and Rupert Spira have all had one-person shows here. The Gallery values traditional studio pottery, such as that produced by Clive Bowen and Lisa Hammond, while we will also embrace subversive, narrative works from artists such as the brilliant Philip Eglin, Stephen Bird, Paul Scott and Dawn Youll. Beautiful, quiet work with rich surfaces and subtle glazes are appreciated too, exemplified by the porcelain still-life groups of Kirsten Coelho.

The Scottish Gallery in recent years has produced several international glass presentations, including *Spectrum* in 2014, *Cutting Edge: Hungarian Glass* in 2015 and, more recently, *Connections* in conjunction with the Contemporary Glass Society. The aim has been to bring unusual, distinctive work to The Gallery and highlight local talent within a wider international context. We have long-serving artists such as Colin Reid, who has exhibited with us since 1979. An artist at the height of his powers, he specialises in kiln-formed glass and is able to either amplify colour or create grand illusions through reflection and refraction. On a smaller scale, Andrea Walsh creates exquisitely made vessels, predominantly in glass and ceramic. Bob Crooks is one of the UK's most talented glass-blowers, whilst the American artist Dante Marioni is considered one of the world's finest living glass-blowers. Both artists use ancient Italian glass-blowing techniques such as reticello and cane work. As a strong contrast, the Edinburgh-based visual artist Harry Morgan combines Venetian murrine techniques with concrete or metal, creating a visual dichotomy between beauty and brutality. His work is not traditional glassmaking but a new application of the medium; creating powerful and bold architectural statements.

Our jewellery is underpinned by talent from the Scottish art colleges; Edinburgh and Glasgow in particular have provided us with generations of artist-makers. Wendy Ramshaw, with her signature ringsets, is still one of the UK's most iconic jewellers and has become synonymous with The Gallery through a series of memorable one-person exhibitions such as *Room of Dreams*, 2002. In 2017, The Gallery presented *Wendy Ramshaw and David Watkins: A Life's Partnership* at Collect (the international fair for contemporary objects) in the Saatchi

Gallery, London and was awarded Outstanding Gallery Presentation. In The Gallery, precious jewellery is shown alongside work made from non-traditional materials and it is our overarching understanding of the diverse world of contemporary jewellery that provides the display context and intellectual rationale. Malcolm Appleby has been associated with The Gallery since the late 1980s, a master engraver and maverick whose work continues to inspire and give joy to many. Scotland has always been a traditional heartland for master craftsmen in the field of metalwork, and despite the decline in traditional silverware, artists such as Malcolm Appleby, Michael Lloyd and Adrian Hope continue to excite. Adi Toch inhabits the next generation of artists using metal as their medium by creating new, diverse forms with patinated or textured surfaces and whose enigmatic, award-winning work also encompasses sound.

Andrea Geile is a sculptor with whom we have collaborated for over ten years. Working in corten steel, she produces artworks in both monumental and domestic scale, including garden sculpture, and she has completed several large-scale public commissions over the last few years. Her work has often defined our garden space. Jim Partridge and Liz Walmsley have been in partnership since the 1990s, producing both large-scale public art and also domestic furniture in predominantly English oak, which is then scorched and burnished and is deeply familiar to visitors to our gallery and external events.

We have illustrated two tapestry weavers in this publication: Jo Barker and Sara Brennan. Both were trained at Edinburgh College of Art, have work in numerous public collections, have studios in Edinburgh and are considered world-class in their field.

Our final chapter gives us three artists who work with willow, an ancient, traditional craft which has seen a renaissance in recent years. Artists working in this medium bring a warm, human dimension into The Gallery and provide a reminder of our links to the past; ancient hand craft skills bring a sense of calm as an antidote to our fast-paced lives. There are three artists working with willow who have become synonymous with The Gallery: Lise Bech and Lizzie Farey both live and work in Scotland whilst Joe Hogan is from the West Coast of Ireland. All three grow their own willow and all of them make both traditional baskets and fine art works which stem from their individual approach to the material and comes from a deep connection to the land.

The following pages contain a glimpse of the hundreds of artists we have shown over the years, and create a visual snapshot of the quality of work to be discovered in our gallery.

Kirsten Coelho working in her Adelaide studio, 2015. Photo: Tony Kearney

The World of Objects

# Ceramics

Cat.89, Stephen Bird,
Korean Man With Jug, 2015,
Korean buncheong clay with
pigment and glaze,
H35 x W15.5 x D15 cms

## STEPHEN BIRD (b.1964)

Stephen Bird was born in The Potteries, trained at Duncan of Jordanstone in Dundee and, making his home and a huge international reputation from Sydney, he remains aloof from any artist pigeon-hole. He works with both paint and clay and has also undertaken a number of site-specific sculpture commissions. Bird's influences and interests include English figure and slipware traditions and paintings and artefacts culled from his extensive travels through India, Asia and Australia. His use of words, collage and found objects as part of the final work, results in powerful multi-dimensional imagery which reflect on the global, transcultural nature of myths and ceramic archetypes.

'I was not surprised to discover that Stephen was born in Stoke-on-Trent. Staffordshire pottery figures, Toby jugs and Commemorative plates seem to have migrated to Australia with Bird and taken up citizenship – murder and mayhem in the outback, shoot-outs in the Eucalypts, sex in the Pandanas.' — Roger Law, 2013

Public Collections include:
National Gallery of Australia, Canberra, Australia
National Museums Scotland, Edinburgh
National Museums Northern Ireland
Art Gallery of South Australia, Adelaide
Artbank Sydney, Australia
Deakin University Art Gallery and Museums,
Melbourne, Australia
Aberdeen Art Gallery and Museums, Scotland
Dundee Art Gallery and Museum, Scotland

Stephen Bird in his studio in Alexandria, Sydney, 2016

Clive Bowen, selection of slipware, Devon, 2010. Photo: Roop Johnstone

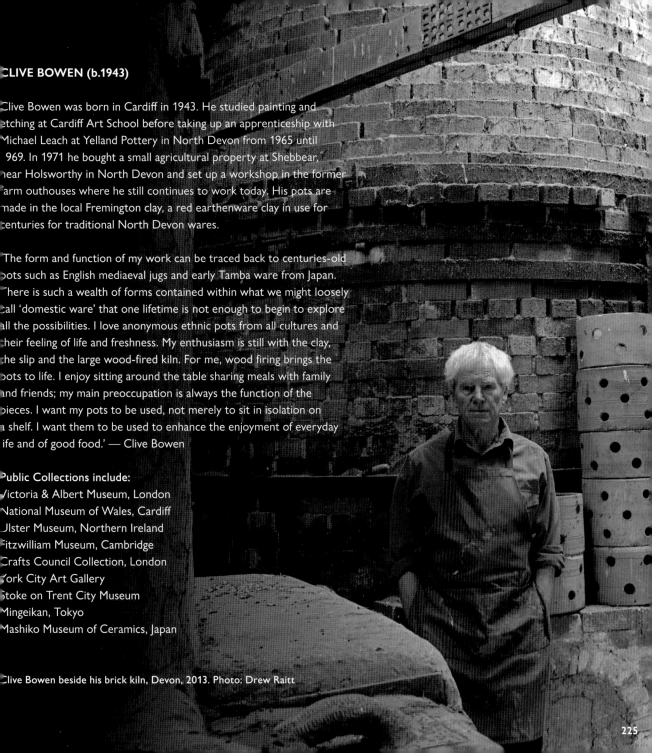

# CLIVE BOWEN (b.1943)

Clive Bowen was born in Cardiff in 1943. He studied painting and etching at Cardiff Art School before taking up an apprenticeship with Michael Leach at Yelland Pottery in North Devon from 1965 until 1969. In 1971 he bought a small agricultural property at Shebbear, near Holsworthy in North Devon and set up a workshop in the former farm outhouses where he still continues to work today. His pots are made in the local Fremington clay, a red earthenware clay in use for centuries for traditional North Devon wares.

The form and function of my work can be traced back to centuries-old pots such as English mediaeval jugs and early Tamba ware from Japan. There is such a wealth of forms contained within what we might loosely call 'domestic ware' that one lifetime is not enough to begin to explore all the possibilities. I love anonymous ethnic pots from all cultures and their feeling of life and freshness. My enthusiasm is still with the clay, the slip and the large wood-fired kiln. For me, wood firing brings the pots to life. I enjoy sitting around the table sharing meals with family and friends; my main preoccupation is always the function of the pieces. I want my pots to be used, not merely to sit in isolation on a shelf. I want them to be used to enhance the enjoyment of everyday life and of good food.' — Clive Bowen

Public Collections include:
Victoria & Albert Museum, London
National Museum of Wales, Cardiff
Ulster Museum, Northern Ireland
Fitzwilliam Museum, Cambridge
Crafts Council Collection, London
York City Art Gallery
Stoke on Trent City Museum
Mingeikan, Tokyo
Mashiko Museum of Ceramics, Japan

Clive Bowen beside his brick kiln, Devon, 2013. Photo: Drew Raitt

# ADAM BUICK (b.1978)

Adam Buick studied Archaeology and Anthropology at
Lampeter University before enrolling in Art School in 2003
and undertaking a Ceramics and Design course in 2004.
His studio is situated at Llanferran on the north coast of
the St. David's Peninsula, Wales.

'My work uses a single pure jar form as a canvas to map
my observations from an ongoing study of my surroundings.
I incorporate stone and locally dug clay into my work to
create a narrative, one that conveys a unique sense of place.
The unpredictable nature of each jar comes from the inclusions
and their metamorphosis during firing. This individuality and
tension between materials speaks of the human condition
and how the landscape shapes us as individuals. I was inspired
by archaeological theories that the Menhirs of prehistory are
a veneration of the landscapes that surrounds them. With
my site-specific work I too am venerating the landscape.
By placing a Jar at a particular location within the landscape
I hope that it will make us look beyond the object to its
surroundings.' — Adam Buick

**Public Collections include:**
Crafts Council Collection, London
Chatsworth House, Derbyshire
Oriental Museum, Durham
National Museum Wales, Cardiff

Adam Buick, Pembrokeshire, 2016

Opposite: Cat.90, Adam Buick, Large Moon Jar, 2016,
stoneware with landscape inclusions, H40 x W33 cms

## KIRSTEN COELHO (b.1966)

Kirsten Coelho trained in Adelaide at the South Australian School of Art where, after a brief period living in the UK, she also completed a Masters in Visual Art. Kirsten now works from a studio at her home in Adelaide, South Australia.

'*Cannister, Bottle and Cup* draws on an ongoing fascination with nineteenth century migration and exploration into Australia. With objects there is the possibility of creating narratives – each piece points to an associated purpose, imbued with multiple social and cultural histories and interpretations. There is also the reference to the abstractions found in the everyday, the chip of an enamel mug, the scratched paint of a car or the ageing surfaces of industrial chimneys. I have always felt drawn to the abstract in art – the potential for understanding through an ambiguous and imperceptible type of knowing. Ceramic objects communicate on many levels and it is these possibilities of engagement and response that I find compelling. The intersection of form, colour, tone and light are the constant drivers.'
— Kirsten Coelho, 2015

Public Collections include:
Chatsworth House, Derbyshire, UK
National Gallery of Australia
Newcastle Art Gallery, Australia
Queensland Art Gallery, Australia
GOMA, Australia

Kirsten Coelho working in her Adelaide studio, 2015. Photo: Tony Kearney

Opposite: Cat.91, Kirsten Coelho, Canister, Bottle and Cup, 2015, porcelain, matt white glaze, banded iron oxide and saturated iron glaze. Left Canister, H13 x D7cms / Middle Bottle, H22 x D11cms / Right Cup, H8.5 x D8.5cms. Photo: Grant Hancock

## PHILIP EGLIN (b.1959)

Philip Eglin studied at Staffordshire Polytechnic and the Royal College of Art, London. He was winner of the prestigious Jerwood Prize for Applied Arts in 1996. The Scottish Gallery has exhibited Eglin's work since the 1980's. His post-modern aesthetic draws on many sources from popular culture and ceramic history through to high art and from Gothic Madonnas to Abstract Expressionist painters of the 1950s. Frequent use of graffitti elements carry playful references to street culture and his sculptures often incorporate pieces moulded from everyday objects such as coke bottles or throw-away plastic. He works in both the figurative and the abstract, using his forms as a canvas or vehicle for whatever narrative he is exploring. He also creates garnitures or installations of both small scale and larger works.

'I see myself as continuing a strong ceramic tradition of borrowing ideas, for both form and surface, from examples found in other media. I enjoy being flippant and subversive, making fusions of seemingly disparate historical and contemporary subjects in an attempt to achieve a balance between the high and the lowbrow, the reverent and the irreverent, the sophisticated and the crude.'
— Philip Eglin

Public Collections include:
Victoria & Albert Museum, London
Fitzwilliam Museum, Cambridge
National Museums Scotland, Edinburgh
Liverpool Museum and Art Gallery
Birmingham Museum and Art Gallery
Mint Museum, North Carolina, USA
Stedelijk Museum, The Netherlands
Middlesbrough Institute of Modern Art
Museum of Fine Arts, Houston, Texas, USA

Philip Eglin in his studio in Wales, 2017. Photo: Oliver Eglin

Opposite: Work in progress for The Scottish Gallery, 2017

# LISA HAMMOND
## MBE (b.1956)

Fascinated with pots from a young age, Lisa consolidated her training in studio pottery in Medway, Kent. She set up Greenwich Pottery Workshop in 1980 alongside teaching at Goldsmiths College for some thirteen years, where committed students and staff helped her to pioneer the use of soda glaze in the UK. Lisa's work embraces the extensive range of thrown functional ware for the preparation, cooking and serving of food. It is immensely important to her that this work is used in daily life. As well as her functional ware, she has always made a range of work that is more individual and playful. The development of these pieces is a result of the time Lisa spent in Japan, making, firing, and exhibiting. Her forms are strong, fluid and unfussy and are intended to retain a suggestion of the soft plasticity of the clay.

'Alongside exploring new forms in my pots, it's the nature of the firing process and its variability that keeps me focused and driven to develop new work after forty years.' — Lisa Hammond, 2016

Lisa Hammond outside her Maze Hill Pottery Studio, London

Opposite: Cat.92, Lisa Hammond, Large Tsubo, 2016, soda fired stoneware, poured white shino and ash runs on black clay, H40 x W32 cms

## DR PAUL SCOTT (b.1953)

'Using the surfaces of transferware, my work has always reflected the contemporary world we live in. As every twenty first century consumer of daily news is aware, the planet appears to be in a perilous state, with wars, shifting refugee populations and environmental degradation brought about by our insatiable greed for resources. Over the years, my artworks have commemorated and examined a range of issues, from the Foot and Mouth crisis to the impact of energy extraction and production on our environment… I have inserted nuclear and coal fired power stations as well as wind turbines into pastoral landscapes, exploratory oil rigs in pristine arctic locations – and placed landscapes with fracking rigs onto cracked platters.

In March 2011, the Fukushima Daiichi nuclear power plant in Japan was enveloped by tidal waves following the Tōhoku earthquake and tsunami. The ensuing events cut power to water-cooling pumps and nuclear fuel rods melted down, creating the largest nuclear disaster since Chernobyl in 1986. Scott's Cumbrian Blue(s) Fukushima series commemorates the event. All works have been made on Willow pattern platters made in Japan. Although the Willow Pattern was originally made in late eighteenth century Staffordshire to imitate Chinese porcelain wares, it is a jumbled confection of designs with decorative details incorporating elements not only of Chinese porcelain but also Japanese Imari ware. It has been produced all over the world. I collaged an erased piece of an old English Willow pattern platter (c.1840) into the scene. I removed the original print and replaced it with an in-glaze print after Katsushika Hokusai's woodblock print 'The Great Wave off Kanagawa (c.1830). The nuclear power plant can be seen behind garden buildings.' — Paul Scott, 2016

Public Collections include:
Victoria & Albert Museum, London
National Museums Scotland, Edinburgh
New York Historical Society, USA
Aberystwyth University, Gallery & Museum, Wales
Potteries Museum, Stoke on Trent
National Museum of Wales, Cardiff

Paul Scott working in his studio
and garden in Cumbria, 2016

Scott's Cumbrian Blue(s), Fukushima No. 8, 2016, H30 x W41 cms.
Last Kintsugi platter in the series acquired by Aberystwyth University, Gallery & Museum, 2017

## JULIAN STAIR (b.1955)

Born in Bristol in 1955 to a family of artists and writers, Julian Stair took up pottery at the age of 16 and went on to study at Camberwell School of Art and the Royal College of Art, London, graduating in 1981. Creating powerful, meticulous works of art on both a monumental and intimate scale, Julian's work has gained an international reputation and is held in over 30 collections worldwide. Julian is also a leading historian of English studio ceramics, completing a PhD at the RCA researching the critical origins of English studio pottery. *Quietus: The Vessel, Death and the Human Body* was his last major UK touring exhibition.

Public Collections include:

British Museum, London
Victoria & Albert Museum, London
Fitzwilliam Museum, Cambridge
Grassi Museum, Leipzig, Germany
Hong Kong Museum of Art
Aberystwyth University Ceramic Collection & Archive
National Museum of Wales
Mashiko Museum of Ceramic Art, Japan
Middlesbrough Institute of Modern Art
Kolumba Museum, Cologne, Germany
Mashiko Museum of Ceramic Art, Japan
Museum of Art & Design, New York, USA

Julian Stair in his London studio, 2016. Photo: Matthew Warner

Cat.93, Julian Stair, Two Cups on a Ground, 2017, porcelain, coloured porcelain, clear glaze, valchromat, lime, marble powder and pigment, H17.5 x W20.5 x D10 cms. Photo: Matthew Warner

Cat.94, Julian Stair, Eleven Cups on a Ground, 2017, porcelain, coloured porcelain, clear glaze, valchromat, lime, marble powder and pigment, H18 x W90 x D10 cms.
Photo: Matthew Warner

## DAWN YOULL (b.1977)

Dawn Youll is a ceramicist, originally from Sunderland, now based in Glasgow. She studied ceramics at The Glasgow School of Art, 1999 and later at Cardiff School of Art & Design, graduating with an MA in 2008. Alongside her studio practice she worked in the Scottish film and television industry and is currently Craft Programme Producer for Cove Park, an artists' residency organisation on the west coast of Scotland. Dawn Youll's sculptural practice centres on the exploration of a personal narrative. The urban environment, the studio setting, and the making process itself all play a part in the development of her ornamentally scaled ceramic sculptures. From research gathered she selects and considers form, colour, surface and words as separate elements, gradually allowing them to find comfortable partners and groupings as a body of work develops. Using clay as her chosen medium and traditional ceramic techniques such as modelling, plaster forming, mould making and slip casting, allows her to explore the power of the ceramic ornament as a carrier of narratives, produced throughout history to record and commemorate many aspects of daily life.

The three-legged form in *Be Prepared* reflects that of a camp fire or a simple shelter and is reminiscent of the world of Guiding or Scouting. The gold of the piece references a different and perhaps darker side to self-preservation. The plastic cable tie both binds and grounds the two elements.

**Public Collections include:**
Victoria & Albert Museum, London
Crafts Council Collection, London

Dawn Youll is represented by
Marsden Woo Gallery, London

Dawn Youll in her studio, Glasgow, 2017.
Photo: Colin Tennant

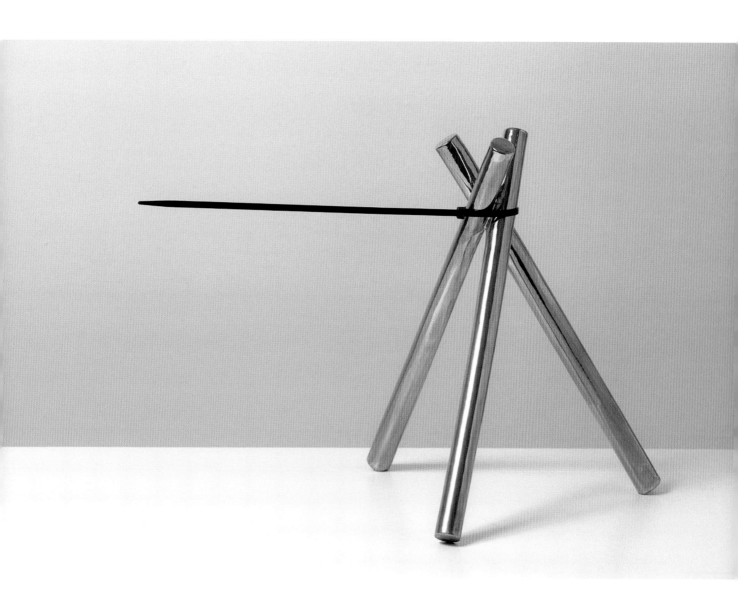

Cat.95, Dawn Youll, Be Prepared, 2014, slip cast earthenware, H26 x D34 cms.
Photo: Philip Sayer, courtesy of Marsden Woo Gallery

Cat.96. Harry Morgan. Blue Box (detail). 2016, concrete and glass,
H40 x W30 x D12 cms. Photo: Shannon Tofts

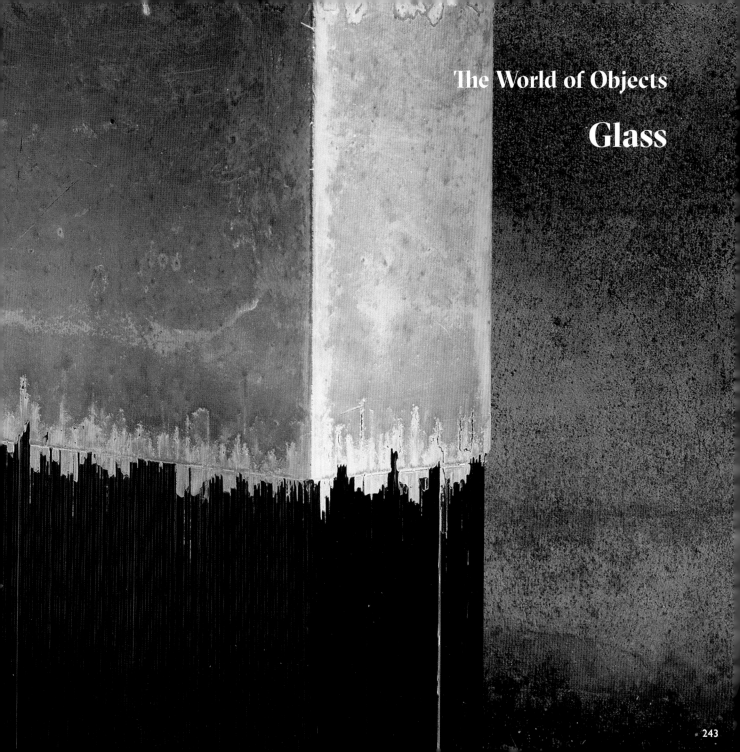

The World of Objects

# Glass

# KATHARINE COLEMAN
## MBE (b.1949)

Katharine Coleman studied glass engraving as a mature student at Morley College, London, with Peter Dreiser from 1984–87. Katharine is a freelance glass engraver and designer currently based in London, who engraves on clear lead crystal forms, overlaid with coloured glass, blown to her design. Once blown and annealed, the top surface of the glass is cut and polished to allow one to see inside the piece, which is then engraved. The engraved decoration reflects and refracts onto the inner surface, creating an illusion of one body floating inside another. The inspiration for her work ranges from natural history to the modern urban landscape.

For many years, I have been interested in the optical properties of glass and how engraving on the glass surface may produce unexpected and fascinating effects on and in the glass itself. I rely heavily on the skills of glassblowers Potter Morgan Glass to realise my designs in colour overlaid crystal and enjoy the challenge of joining hot glass design with cold working. Japanese art and design, the famous engravings of Ernst Haeckel and modern architecture have all informed the subject matter of my work, as has what the American philosopher Thomas Moore so eloquently described as "the beautiful ordinary".

The Haeckel Green Flustra Bowl is inspired by the engravings of Ernst Haeckel, the 19th Century zoologist; whose illustrations of planktons, diatoms and minute plant forms such as the flustra inspired many artists and architects at the turn of the 20th Century.

### Public Collections include:
Broadfield House Glass Museum, Kingswinford
Cheltenham Art Gallery and Museum, Gloucestershire
North Lands Creative Glass Collection, Scotland
Shipley Art Gallery, Gateshead
National Museums Scotland, Edinburgh
Victoria & Albert Museum, London
Kunstsammlungen der Veste Coburg, Germany
The Fitzwilliam Museum, Cambridge
Muzeum Skla Kamenický Senov, Kamenický Senov, Czech Republic
Corning Museum of Glass, New York

Katharine Coleman in her London studio, 2015

Katharine Coleman, Haeckel Green Flustra Bowl, 2012 (Purchased from The Scottish Gallery, 2013),
green glass overlaid on clear lead crystal, cut, polished and wheel engraved, H8 x D16.4 cms. Photo: William Van Esland

## BOB CROOKS (b.1965)

Bob Crooks is one of Britain's leading glass artists. He has established a strong reputation for his exceptional blown glasswork with sophisticated use of colour and technique. Each piece is unique and Bob uses a variety of hot and cold working processes. His work has been exhibited internationally and is held in numerous public collections.

'Bob Crooks works in a highly disciplined daily routine from early till late. The studio must be kept immaculate, the furnace at the right temperature and filled with glass, all the machinery and tools in ship shape. Only then can the excitement of glass blowing begin. Part of the time is devoted to blowing, part to cold working and part to working things out in one's head. Ideas happen all the time with this way of making. Even mistakes can be inspirational and lead to new departures. Athleticism and quick decision making are essential in hot glass blowing. This appeals greatly to Bob Crooks' somewhat impatient nature. The storm and stress of a hot glass workshop are what gets his creative juices flowing, the agitated process in and around the furnace. There is more time for reflection and refinement in the cold working studio. The whole process, with a magic all its own, combines the excitement and danger of heat with the cooler activities of cutting and polishing.' — © Dan Klein, 2006

Public Collections include:
National Museums Scotland, Edinburgh
Victoria & Albert Museum, London
Bristol Museum & Art Gallery
European Museum of Modern Glass, Germany
The Fitzwilliam Museum, Cambridge
Mobile Museum of Art, Alabama
Walker Art Gallery, Liverpool Museums
Ruskin Glass Centre, Stourbridge
Manchester Metropolitan University
The Sainsbury Collection, Norwich
Standard Life Art Collection, Edinburgh
British Council Collection, London

Bob Crooks, Giverny (detail), 2016. Photo: Ian Jackson

Opposite: Bob Crooks, Giverny, 2016, hand blown glass incorporating hand pulled canes, H41 x W42 x D17 cms. Photo: Ian Jackson. Purchased from The Scottish Gallery, 2016

# DANTE MARIONI (b.1964)

Dante Marioni was born into a family of glassblowers and from an early age he spent summers at Pilchuck Glass School in Washington, USA, before studying glassblowing at The Glass Eye, Washington. Dante's passion for glass was also stimulated by the artists that he came into contact with from the American studio glass movement in San Francisco. His work reveals combinations of classical Greek, Italian, and modern forms using opaque and transparent colours. His amphoras, vases and ewers are derived from Greek and Etruscan prototypes, yet they are imaginatively and sometimes whimsically reinterpreted. Dante Marioni is considered a master of glassblowing and his work is held in numerous private and public collections worldwide.

'I have never really been in love with all the obvious qualities of glass. I am more in love with the process and the traditions, age-old and of the contemporary studio variety. Form is always my primary concern; light manipulation and colour are almost an afterthought.' — Dante Marioni, 2014

Selected Awards:
Elected to the College of Fellows, American Craft Council, New York, 2012
Outstanding Achievement in Glass, Urban Glass Award, New York, 1997
Young Americans, American Craft Museum, New York, 1988

Public Collections include:
Victoria & Albert Museum, London
New Zealand National Museum, Auckland
National Gallery of Victoria, Melbourne, Australia
National Museum of Stockholm, Sweden
Japanese National Museum of Modern Art, Tokyo, Japan
American Museum of Art and Design, New York
Corning Museum of Glass, New York
North Lands Creative Glass Collection, Scotland

Dante Marioni in his Seattle studio, 2012. Photo: Birthe Piontek

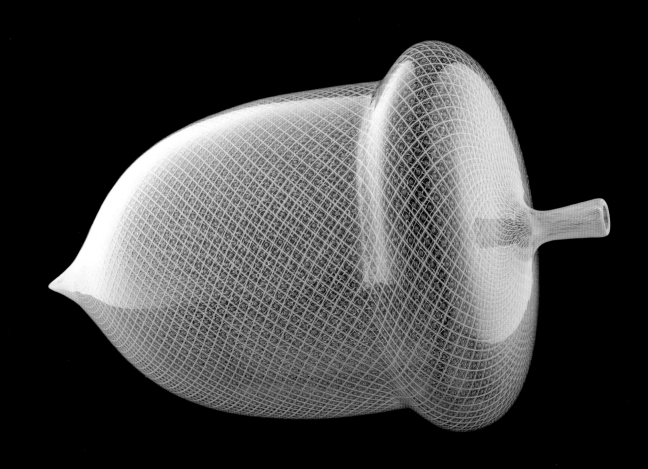

Cat.97, Dante Marioni, White Reticello Acorn, 2010, blown glass, 30.5 x 25.5 cms. Photo: William Van Esland

## JAMES MASKREY (b.1967)

James Maskrey originally trained as an apprentice and
worked for seven years at a hot glass studio in Dorset.
In 1997 he embarked on a three dimensional design degree
in glass at the University for the Creative Arts, Farnham,
Surrey. In 2001 he joined the glass and ceramics department
at the University of Sunderland before completing his
Masters in 2004. He continues to work for the University,
specialising in hot glass and is considered a master glass
blower. He combines hot glass techniques with his love
of storytelling.

Public Collections include
Victoria & Albert Museum, London
National Museums Scotland, Edinburgh
Crafts Council, London
Perth Museum and Art Gallery, Scotland
Captain Cook Memorial Museum, UK
North Lands Creative Glass Collection, Scotland
Crystallex Collection, Czech Republic
University of Sunderland, UK
Manchester Metropolitan University, UK
University for the Creative Arts, Farnham

'Last of the Silver Darlings is part of a small body of work
recognising the herring fishing industry of the North East
coast of Scotland. Once a booming trade, the fish stocks
became depleted through a mixture of over-fishing and
current change; leaving many abandoned stations and
harbours that litter the North East coast. These pieces
have been inspired by time spent at North Lands
Creative Glass, based in the village of Lybster, Caithness.'
— James Maskrey, 2015

James Maskrey, Shackleton's Scrimshaw, 2014
Photo: Colin Davison

Opposite: The Last of the Silver Darlings,
2014, free-blown glass jar and lid with
canemara and incalmo technique, hot
sculpted fish and finial, H49 x D25 cms.
Photo: David Williams. Acquired for the
National Museums Scotland, Edinburgh, 2015

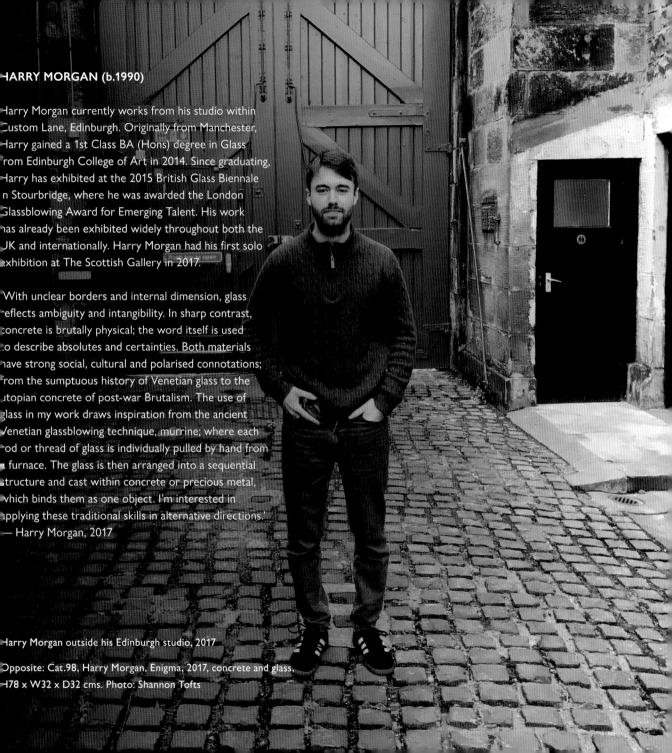

# HARRY MORGAN (b.1990)

Harry Morgan currently works from his studio within Custom Lane, Edinburgh. Originally from Manchester, Harry gained a 1st Class BA (Hons) degree in Glass from Edinburgh College of Art in 2014. Since graduating, Harry has exhibited at the 2015 British Glass Biennale in Stourbridge, where he was awarded the London Glassblowing Award for Emerging Talent. His work has already been exhibited widely throughout both the UK and internationally. Harry Morgan had his first solo exhibition at The Scottish Gallery in 2017.

'With unclear borders and internal dimension, glass reflects ambiguity and intangibility. In sharp contrast, concrete is brutally physical; the word itself is used to describe absolutes and certainties. Both materials have strong social, cultural and polarised connotations; from the sumptuous history of Venetian glass to the utopian concrete of post-war Brutalism. The use of glass in my work draws inspiration from the ancient Venetian glassblowing technique, murrine; where each rod or thread of glass is individually pulled by hand from a furnace. The glass is then arranged into a sequential structure and cast within concrete or precious metal, which binds them as one object. I'm interested in applying these traditional skills in alternative directions.'
— Harry Morgan, 2017

Harry Morgan outside his Edinburgh studio, 2017

Opposite: Cat.98, Harry Morgan, Enigma, 2017, concrete and glass, H78 x W32 x D32 cms. Photo: Shannon Tofts

## COLIN REID (b.1953)

Colin Reid studied at St Martins College of Art and
Stourbridge School of Art; initially training as a scientific
glassblower. He is an acknowledged master of cast glass
as an artistic medium and has work represented in over
50 collections worldwide. His sources of inspiration are
numerous, but each work uses the qualities of glass
– transparency, refraction and reflection – to extraordinary,
dynamic effect. In 2012, The Duke & Duchess of Buccleuch
commissioned Colin Reid to make a site specific piece
for Bowhill and to make four glass awards for the Walter
Scott Prize for Historical Fiction. Lund Humphries published
a monograph on the work of Colin Reid in 2013 to coincide
with his retrospective exhibition at the Cheltenham
Art Gallery & Museum in 2014.

Public Collections include:
Victoria & Albert Museum, London
Crafts Council, London
Broadfield House Glass Museum, Stourbridge
National Museums Wales, Cardiff
National Museums Liverpool, Merseyside
The Fitzwilliam Museum, Cambridge
National Museums Scotland, Edinburgh
Museo de Arte en Vidrio de Alcorcón, Madrid, Spain
Glasmuseet Ebeltoft, Ebeltoft, Denmark
Musée des Arts Décoratifs, Paris, France
Glass Art Fund, Strasbourg, France

Colin Reid, Walter Scott Prize for Historical Fiction (detail),
2012–2013, kiln cast glass. Photo: John Heseltine, 2012

Opposite: Colin Reid, Ring of Aqua, 2016, kilncast glass,
H41 x W42 x D2–7 cms. Purchased from The Scottish Gallery, 2016

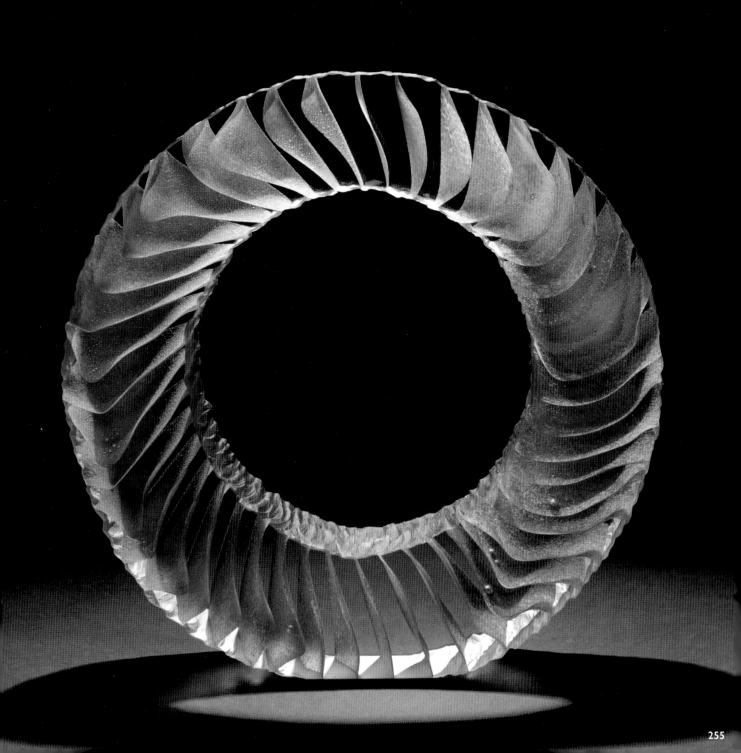

## ANDREA WALSH (b.1974)

Andrea Walsh studied fine art at Staffordshire University before completing an MA in glass design at Edinburgh College of Art in 2001. In 2009 Andrea was awarded a residency with Wedgwood from the British Ceramics Biennial, which led to her first series of faceted boxes. Andrea lives and works in Edinburgh.

'I have focused on glass and ceramics over the past ten years, creating box and vessel forms which celebrate and investigate the qualities that these ancient and alchemic materials share. Most recently I have worked on a series of contained boxes, where individual ceramic and metal boxes are held, almost cradled, inside a glass container. Each box is polished smooth and rounded in shape, and each container is a finely cast shell of varying translucency and opacity – revealing different qualities and references within each unique piece.'
— Andrea Walsh

**Public Collections include**
Victoria & Albert Museum, London
National Museums Scotland, Edinburgh

Andrea Walsh in her Edinburgh studio, 2011

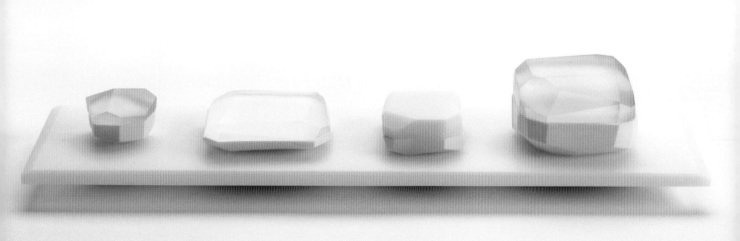

Andrea Walsh, Collection of Faceted Boxes, 2009–2013, fine bone china and glass, W34 cms
Photo: Shannon Tofts. Acquired for National Museums Scotland, Edinburgh, 2014

Detail of work in progress from Julie Blyfield's Adelaide studio showing hand-raised silver cups and paper maquettes, 2015. Photo: Grant Hancock

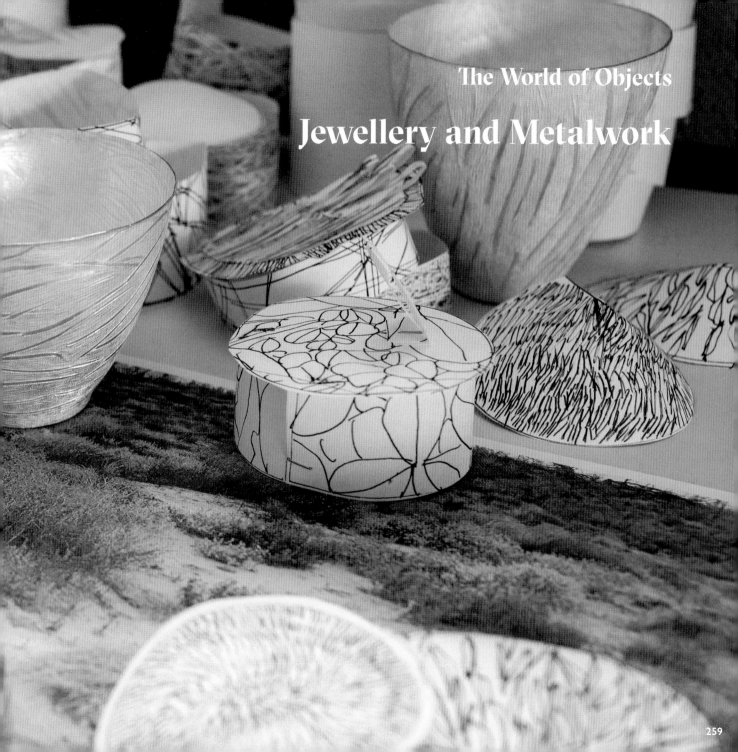

## MALCOLM APPLEBY
### MBE (b.1946)

The Scottish Gallery honoured Malcolm Appleby's
70th birthday in January 2016, which marked over
50 years of a creative tour de force. Malcolm Appleby
has dedicated his artistic practice primarily to engraving
and pushing the boundaries of metalwork; constant
experimentation has made him a master of his craft
and in 2014 he received an MBE for his outstanding
contribution to the arts.

The Gallery has been associated with Malcolm Appleby
since the 1970s; the many facets of his work has brought
joy to many, each piece sold marking the beginning
of a journey of discovery around this senior artist.

'Malcolm now lives in a purpose-built workshop and
home, designed to his own specification. It stands in
9 acres of ground; some now cultivated with tatties and
vegetables, a wonderous array of herbs, and a young
orchard. Living above the shop allows him to be flexible
and indulge his incredible energy and dedication to his
craft. The Post Office is nearby, the travelling bank visits
weekly, and the proximity of the A9 gives easy access
to all points North and South… An air of contentment
and tranquility pervades, but Malcolm is not to be
found relaxing. The work continues apace, constantly
developing and progressing…'

— Christine Rew, Aberdeen Art Gallery & Museums
(Malcolm Appleby, Designer and Engraver, 1998)

Public Collections include:
Aberdeen Art Gallery & Museums
Ashmolean Museum of Art & Archaeology,
University of Oxford
Birmingham City Art Gallery
British Museum, London
Fitzwilliam Museum, Cambridge
Goldsmiths' Company, London
The Hunterian, University of Glasgow
National Museums Scotland, Edinburgh
Perth Museum & Art Gallery
Royal Armouries, Tower of London
Victoria & Albert Museum, London

Photograph of Malcolm Appleby by David Eustace, 2015

Above: Cat.99, Malcolm Appleby, Hurricane Force 12, 2016, enamel, sterling silver cast from engraving, approx H7 x W12 x D10 cms, enamel by Jane Short signed and dated on base Malcolm Appleby 04.11.15. Photo: Philippa Swann

Opposite: Cat.100, Malcolm Appleby, Chains (detail), 2017, silver chains, 18ct yellow chains, various designs with stamped patterns

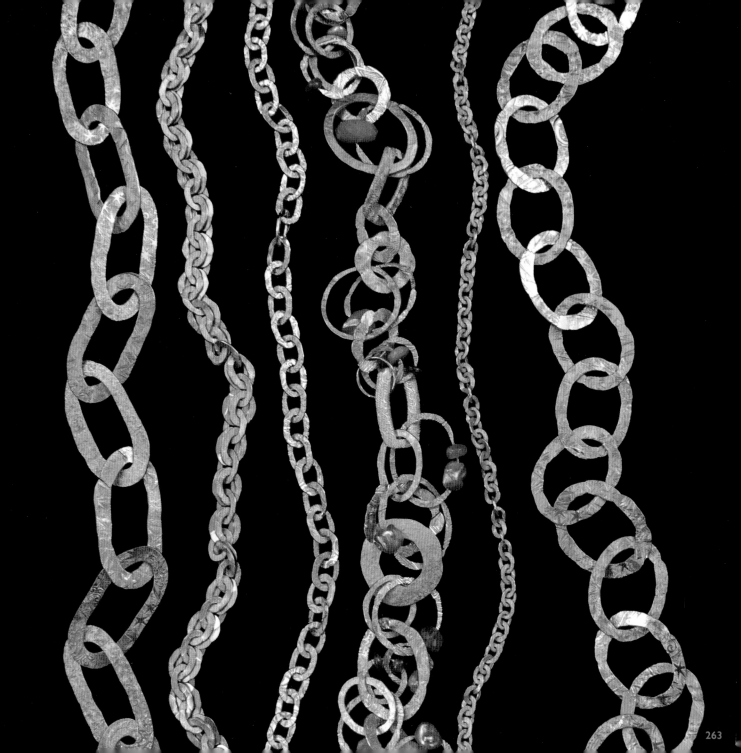

Julie Blyfield at her design bench in her studio,
Adelaide, 2015. Photo: Grant Hancock

## JULIE BLYFIELD (b.1957)

Julie Blyfield makes jewellery, small-scale vessels and sculptural objects in her studio nestling in the garden of her home in Adelaide, South Australia. Inspired by the botanical landscape in Australia, Julie's favoured medium of expression is silver. This she uses in its softer pure form as well as in its stronger alloyed form – sterling silver. Her jewellery and vessels are characterised by seductive textured surfaces created using traditional silversmithing techniques such as hammering, chasing, punching and piercing. Rhythmical repetition is a key element of both her design process and her aesthetic and the use of colour is also apparent. Following the traumatising Australian bushfires of 2007, Blyfield echoed the scorched colour and searing heat with enamel paint and startling glints of gold and silver set against charred blacks and ash greys.

'My work is inspired by the botanical landscape in Australia, which I interpret in my metal work using the technique of 'metal raising' and 'chasing'. I enjoy exploring and collecting plant specimens from rich and diverse environments such as the Simpson Desert in the north of South Australia and further south around the coast of Kangaroo Island. Working with both pure silver and sterling silver as my preferred choice of material, I texture the surface to create individual pieces in the form of vessels and also more sculptural pieces. During the making process, I enjoy the way the metal 'moves and shifts' in almost unpredictable ways to create the organic forms which shimmer with the silver textures or colours derived from nature.'
— Julie Blyfield, 2016

**Public Collections include:**
Aberdeen Art Galleries and Museums, Aberdeen, UK
Art Gallery of Western Australia, Perth, Australia
National Gallery of Australia, Canberra, Australia
National Museums Scotland, Edinburgh, UK
Victoria & Albert Museum, London

Cat.101, Julie Blyfield, Quench Cups, 2015, oxidised silver and silver, largest: H8 x D8.3 cms. Photo: Grant Hancock

## SUSAN CROSS (b.1964)

Susan Cross has lived and worked in Edinburgh since 1989. In 2017, she was the only British jeweller to be selected for the prestigious SCHMUCK 2017, Munich in recognition of excellence, innovation, commitment and significant contribution to the field of jewellery. She was also shortlisted for the Jerwood Applied Arts Award for jewellery in 2007. Susan Cross is a senior lecturer at the prestigious Jewellery and Silversmithing department at Edinburgh College of Art.

'A breadth of interests and ideas continues to fuel and underpin the development of the jewellery that I make. Each work is carefully composed and every phase is intensely considered. Drawing is an integral part of this creative process; a thoughtful and responsive activity thus ensuring freshness and spontaneity. The complete integration with my life imbues my work with a depth and authenticity belied by its apparent simplicity. As a jeweller, I aim to explore the sensuality of the body through the tactility of the materials. My work enables me to communicate an aspect of myself to those who choose to wear it, articulating my creative energy, allowing the wearer to interpret it at an individual level.'
— Susan Cross

Public Collections include:
Victoria & Albert Museum, London
National Museums Scotland, Edinburgh
Crafts Council, London
Worshipful Company of Goldsmiths, London
Birmingham Museum & Art Gallery
Edinburgh Royal Infirmary

Susan Cross in her Edinburgh studio.
Photo: Michael Wolchover

Left: Cat.102, Susan Cross, Composition Brooch with Gold Hoop, 2010, oxidised silver, Korean textile, 18ct gold, H8 x W8 cms
Right: Cat.103, Susan Cross, Enclosure, brooch, 2009, oxidised silver and thread, H2.2 x W7.5 x D6.5 cms

## KOJI HATAKEYAMA (b.1956)

Koji Hatakeyama was born in Takaoka, Toyama Prefecture, an area renowned for the ancient art of metal casting and he graduated from Kanazawa College of Arts and Crafts Department of Metalwork in 1980. Koji's exquisitely made bronze boxes reveal a gold or silver interior. In the western world, his boxes are considered sculptures and in Japan, his boxes have an important function as part of the Japanese tea ceremony. He creates enigmatic, patinated surfaces which represent the landscape, evoking a timeless quality.

'I create contained vessels; I try to convey the sense that something is concealed or hidden within. I try to provoke a sense of the spiritual world in my bronze boxes. The patterns and facets I create on the outside are a direct response to the landscape. I find that when using gold or silver leaf within the interiors, there is a sense of enlightenment when opening the lid, my intention is to enter a different world, a different place. This place has no darkness. My consciousness is veiled in bronze.'
— Koji Hatakeyama

Public Collections include:
Victoria & Albert Museum, London
National Museums Scotland, Edinburgh
Aberdeen Art Gallery and Museum, Aberdeen
Birmingham Museums and Art Gallery
Philadelphia Museum of Art, USA
The Ashmolean Museum, Oxford
National Museum of Victoria, Melbourne, Australia
Denmark Royal Family, Copenhagen, Denmark
National Museum of Modern Art, Tokyo, Japan
The Japan Foundation, Tokyo, Japan
Takaoka City Museum, Toyama, Japan

Koji Hatakeyama in his studio,
Takaoka Toyama Prefecture Japan, 2014.
Photo: Sekai Bunka Publishing Inc.

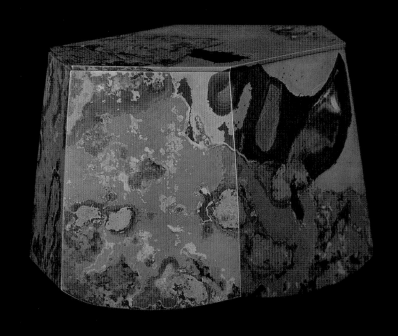

Cat.104, Koji Hatakeyama, Six Faces, 2010, cast bronze, platinum leaf interior,
H18 x W14.5 x D11.5 cms. Photo: Stephen Dunn

## NEL LINSSEN (1935–2016)

The Dutch artist Nel Linssen always took an intuitive
approach to her jewellery made from paper and
was considered a pioneer of modern jewellery. The
relationship between wearer and viewer is paramount
in her work. While the wearer is aware of the sensuous
nature and movement of the jewellery, the viewer
is drawn to the constant visual changes to the work
wrought by the slightest movement of the body. The
Scottish Gallery celebrated Nel Linssen's 80th birthday
with a special exhibition in 2015.

Nel Linssen, Paper Necklace, 2015,
reinforced paper and elastic thread, L60 cms.
Acquired by Aberdeen Art Gallery and Museums, 2016

Public Collections include:
Museum of Modern Art, Arnhem
Stedelijk Museum, Amsterdam
National Museums Scotland, Edinburgh
Aberdeen Art Gallery and Museums
National Galleries of Australia, Canberra
Victoria & Albert Museum, London
Handwerkspflege Bayern, Munich
Kunstgewerbe Museum, Berlin
Cooper-Hewitt Museum, New York
Museum of Applied Art, Oslo
Musée des Arts Decoratifs, Montreal
Brooklyn Museum, New York
Fonds National d'Arts Contemporain, Paris
The National Gallery of Victoria, Melbourne
The Museum of Fine Arts, Houston, USA

## GENEVIEVE HOWARD (b.1992)

'My current work challenges the idea of making music into visual and three dimensional forms. Being a musician myself, I have played and listened to music from a young age. The possibility of translating a piece of music that is personal into a tactile and wearable medium excites me.' — Genevieve Howard, 2017

Genevieve Howard, The Song of the Chanter Neckpiece, 2016, laser cut green Japanese linen paper and elastic cord, H3 x W25 x D25 cms. Photo: Hannah Leavy

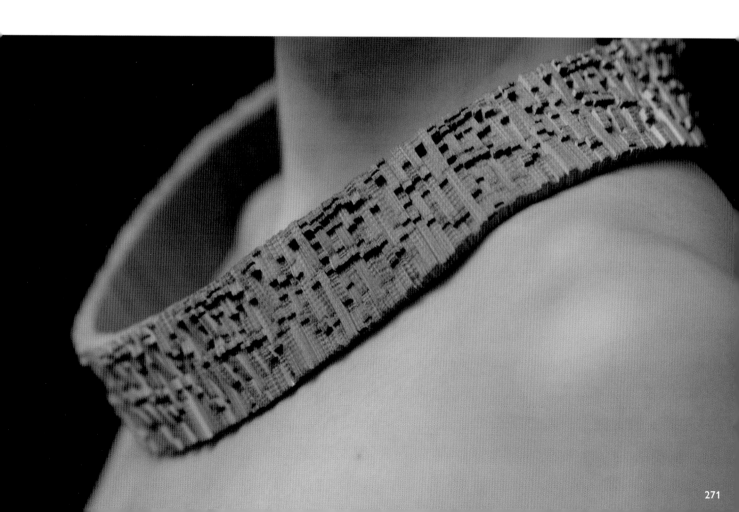

## FELIEKE VAN DER LEEST (b.1968)

Felieke van der Leest is a trained jeweller, graduating from the Rietveld Academie (The Netherlands) in 1996. She has lived and worked in Øystese, Norway since 2008. Living close to a Zoo, her passion for animals probably started in her childhood just like her love for crocheting in textiles. Combining this with precious metals and plastic toy animals, she has developed her own idiom in contemporary jewellery and art objects. Her works are best described as portable miniature sculptures; rich in humorous language.

'When I am working with colour, I feel like a painter. When I am working with metal, I feel like a constructor. And when I am working with toys, I feel like a child.'
— Felieke van der Leest

Public Collections include:
Victoria & Albert Museum, London
CODA Museum, Apeldoorn, the Netherlands
Hiko Mizuno Collection, Tokyo, Japan
Museum of Decorative Arts, Montreal, Canada
Museum of Modern Art, Arnhem, the Netherlands
National Museums Scotland, Edinburgh
Rijksmuseum Amsterdam, Amsterdam, the Netherlands

Felieke van der Leest in her studio in Øystese, Norway

Cat.105, Felieke van der Leest, Half Moonwolf (object with brooch), 2012, crocheted textiles, yellow and white precious metals and mixed materials, H10.5 x W8 x D3.5 cms. Photo: Eddo Hartmann

## MICHAEL LLOYD (b.1950)

Michael Lloyd was born in Salisbury in 1950. He trained first at the Birmingham School of Silversmithing and then at the Royal College of Art under Professor Robert Goodden and Professor Gerald Benney. He has lived and worked in Scotland for over 30 years and is based near Castle Douglas. Michael describes himself as a compulsive maker. Certainly, his beautiful, chased silver and gold vessels illustrate a profound understanding of both material and techniques. Inspired by the natural world, his work becomes, in his own words 'An act of homage, both to our landscape and to our increasingly fragile sense of creativity.'

Public Collections include:
Victoria & Albert Museum, London
Worshipful Company of Goldsmiths, London
National Museums Scotland, Edinburgh
National Archives of Scotland, Edinburgh
Glasgow Museums
Aberdeen Art Gallery & Museum
The Goldsmith's Company, London
Ashmolean Museum, Oxford
Crafts Council Collection, London
Birmingham Museum & Art Gallery
The Fitzwilliam Museum, Cambridge

Michael Lloyd in his garden, Dumfries & Galloway, May 2016

Michael Lloyd, The Beauty of Rain I, 2016, hand raised and chased Britannia silver with gilt interior, H13.5 x D14.5 cms. Acquired by Glasgow Museums, 2017

# JACQUELINE MINA
## OBE (b.1942)

Jacqueline Mina is an important senior figure amongst The Gallery's representation of contemporary jewellers. She had her first solo exhibition with The Gallery in 1993 and The Gallery has continued to show her innovative work ever since.

Jacqueline Mina's technical brilliance, allied with her strong artistic curiosity has resulted in a range of sensuous, understated work, which has a rare aesthetic presence in the field of contemporary gold jewellery. Her superb technical accomplishment in manipulating precious metals is combined with a fine, painterly eye. Sources of inspiration include the Venetian Palazzo Fortuny with its textile drapes; featuring devoré velvet with their etched patterns.

'I aim to achieve an aesthetic result that obscures the technical rigours of its production. I am preoccupied mainly with the surfaces of precious metals (which I always affect in some way before construction begins) and with form – juxtaposing the play of light, reflection, lustre with characteristic angle, curve and line – inspired by an abstraction of nature and art, and particularly of the human form. I am intrigued, too, by the potential for dialogue between inner and outer planes, with random patterns imprisoned within strictly delineated edges, the inclusion of chance, and the visual tension created by the contrast and harmony of all these factors.' — Jacqueline Mina, 2017

Public Collections include:
National Museums Scotland, Edinburgh
Victoria & Albert Museum, London
Cooper–Hewitt, Smithsonian Design Museum, New York
The Crafts Council, London
The Goldsmiths' Company, London
Leeds Museums and Galleries

Jacqueline Mina in her London studio, 2010. Photo: Harriet Logan

Cat.106, Jacqueline Mina, Pleated Necklace, 2016, 18ct yellow gold pleated sheet and twisted square wire, H18 x W15 cms

## GRAINNE MORTON (b.1970)

Originally from Northern Ireland but working from her studio in Edinburgh since 1995, Grainne Morton is a former award winning graduate from Edinburgh College of Art. Collecting obscure and miniature objects is the starting point for Grainne's designs. Through experimentation, objects both formed and found are grouped into 'collections' and housed in handmade boxes or series of work. The various precious, found and vintage materials include pressed flowers, old buttons, shells, pebbles, sea glass, typography and print. To complement these found elements, handmade objects such as enamel work, miniature drawings and punched metal are added to complete the collections.

Public Collections include:
National Museums Scotland, Edinburgh
Crafts Council Collection, London
Montreal Museum of Fine Arts, Canada
Ulster Museum, Belfast

Right: Cat.107, Grainne Morton, Cloud Brooch, 2017, oxidised silver, found objects and semi-precious stone, L9 x W4.5 cms

Opposite: Cat.108, Grainne Morton, Nine Charm Necklace, 2017, oxidised silver and found objects, L26 cms

## PAUL PRESTON (b.1943)

Born in Leeds, Paul Preston a.k.a. the 'Red Mole' originally practiced architecture before becoming a self-taught jeweller. His combination of fine workmanship and imaginative ideas make him one of the most distinctive contemporary British jewellers today. Paul practiced architecture for just two years before retiring to dive the waters round Land's End for crawfish and the recovery of non-ferrous metals from wrecks. He is a self-taught artist who became interested in jewellery after seeing the jewellery of artist and sculptor Breon O'Casey. A large proportion of Paul's work is based on themes from nature, especially birds and fish. This natural world in metal, often has a strong element of fantasy influenced by cartoons and story books, as well as a whimsical, poetic quality. His work is in numerous private and public collections, including the Victoria & Albert Museum, London.

Paul Preston in his studio, West Wales, 2015.
Photo: Jean Thomas

Cat.109, Paul Preston, a selection of rings and earrings, 2015–2016,
white and yellow precious metal with tourmalines and aquamarine

## JACQUELINE RYAN (b.1966)

Jacqueline Ryan spent time at the Fachhochscule in Dusseldorf and after graduating from the Royal College of Art, London in 1991, she moved to Padua, Italy and shared a workshop with Giovanni Corvaja. Jacqueline works exclusively in gold and precious materials to create organic forms characterised by intricate arrangements of repeated elements, bringing to the field a unique voice grounded in the Italian tradition of architecture and design. Jacqueline now has her own workshop in Todi, Italy.

'Most of my pieces are preceded by studies derived from living organisms, marine plants, flowers, or seeds and other found objects with the occasional aid of macrophotography that capture some of the finer-scale qualities more difficult to perceive with the naked eye. Repetition, naturally occurring in nature, is a recurrent theme that runs through much of my work as well as movement in which the composite shapes and forms from which my work is constructed move and sway with the body and sometimes jingle and rattle – quietly giving the work a pleasant tactile dimension and interacting with the wearer so that the piece may be animated and alive. I feel that my work has completed its cycle when it has found its wearer.' — Jacqueline Ryan

Public Collections include:
Victoria & Albert Museum, London
Aberdeen Art Gallery & Museums, Aberdeen
National Museums Scotland, Edinburgh
The Worshipful Company of Goldsmiths, London
Musée des Arts Décoratifs, Paris, France
Museum für Künst und Gewerbe, Hamburg, Germany
Museo degli Argenti, Florence, Italy
The Metropolitan Museum of Art, New York, USA

Jacqueline Ryan in her studio in Todi, Italy, 2015

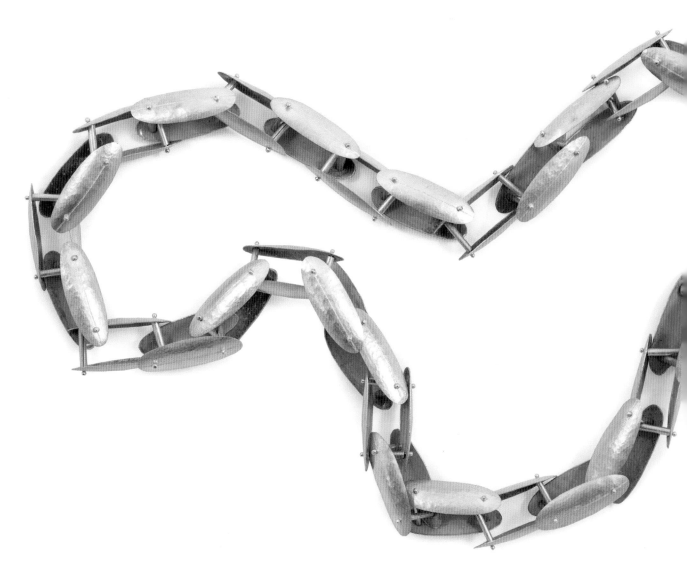

Cat.110, Jacqueline Ryan, Hinged Ovals Necklace (detail),
2016, 18ct gold and enamel, L51 x W1.1 x D1.1 cms

## ADI TOCH (b.1979)

Adi Toch completed her MA at the Cass, London in 2009 following her BA in Jewellery and Objects at Bezalel Art Academy in Jerusalem. She works from her studio in London where she creates enigmatic forms and vessels.

The practice of making vessels and containers fascinates me as it enables me to work both with metal and space as materials, redefining borders between inside and outside. Through my work, I explore the morphological qualities of vessels and the process of embedding functional objects with spirit. I create contemplative work, inviting interaction, and communicating through its tactile essence. The series of patinated bowls explores an experimental technique of chemical colouring, developed in my work in recent years. The compound is applied to the metal and a rich mixture of variegated blues, greens, purples and reds is achieved. The result is a curious finish, which cannot be repeated.' — Adi Toch

Public Collections include:
National Museums Scotland, Edinburgh
Fitzwilliam Museum Cambridge,
Applied Arts Collection
The Jewish Museum, New York
Crafts Council permanent collection, London
The Goldsmiths' Company, London
Turnov Museum, Czech Republic
National Museums Wales, Cardiff

Adi Toch in her London studio. Photo: Isabelle Busnel

Adi Toch, Whispering Vessels, 2016, patinated metal with loose gemstones. Photo: Ben Pollard

**DAVID WATKINS (b.1940) and**
**WENDY RAMSHAW CBE (b.1939)**

David Watkins and Wendy Ramshaw are
a husband and wife team and together, are
considered two of the most iconic figures
in the world of modern jewellery.

Cat.111, David Watkins, Matrix X,
pin, 1993, gold, H16.6 x W8 cms

Cat.112, Wendy Ramshaw, Moon Dreamer,
7 part ringset, 18ct yellow gold with moonstones

Andrea Geile, Level the Field series, 2016, Corten Steel

# The World of Objects

# Sculpture

Andrea Geile, Sibirica Disc, 2004, corten steel, D110 cms. Photo: Michael Wolchover

## ANDREA GEILE (b.1961)

Edinburgh based German artist Andrea Geile trained in print making before studying Visual Art and Sculpture in Hanover. She has been working from her Edinburgh studio since 1996. Her outdoor sculptures are made from everlasting Corten steel, which are often grouped with real plants and relate directly to the surrounding environment. Andrea aims to create a contemporary version of 'Gartenkunst', which challenges existing notions of 'garden art' and 'land sculpture'. She is interested in exploring the interconnection between the landscape, architecture and living plants. Andrea exhibits internationally and her sculptures are in numerous private and public collections.

Public Collections include:
City of Edinburgh Council
The Great Steward of Scotland Dumfries House Trust Collection
The University of Edinburgh
The University of Stirling Art Collection
City of Albany Art Collection, Australia
NHS Tayside

Andrea Geile, Into the Wild, 2015, corten steel, H220 cms

## JIM PARTRIDGE (b.1953) and LIZ WALMSLEY

Jim Partridge and Liz Walmsley are pioneers of modern British furniture and have been associated with The Scottish Gallery since the early 1990's. They both live and work together in Oswestry, in Shropshire near the Welsh border. Jim Partridge studied at John Makepeace's Parnham House School for Craftsmen in Wood in the 1970s, whilst Liz Walmsley's first professional life in the crafts was in the world of ceramics. Since 1986 the couple have worked together designing and making furniture. Their partnership has worked successfully on many architectural projects and environmental commissions. Their studio furniture, much of which is carved from blocks of green oak, often scorched and polished to a lustrous black finish, is in public collections across the world. They have always said that their intention was to make 'work with a strong but quiet presence in the landscape'.

Public collections include:
Crafts Council Collection, London
Contemporary Arts Society, London
Victoria & Albert Museum, London
The British Council
Kyoto Museum of Modern Art, Japan
Boston Museum of Fine Art, USA

Left: Cat.113, Block Stool (detail), 2017, scorched oak, H38 x W85 x D33 cms
Right: Faceted Vessel, 2017, scorched oak, H25 x W36 x D30 cms

Jo Barker, Lime Glow (detail) tapestry in progress on the loom, 2011

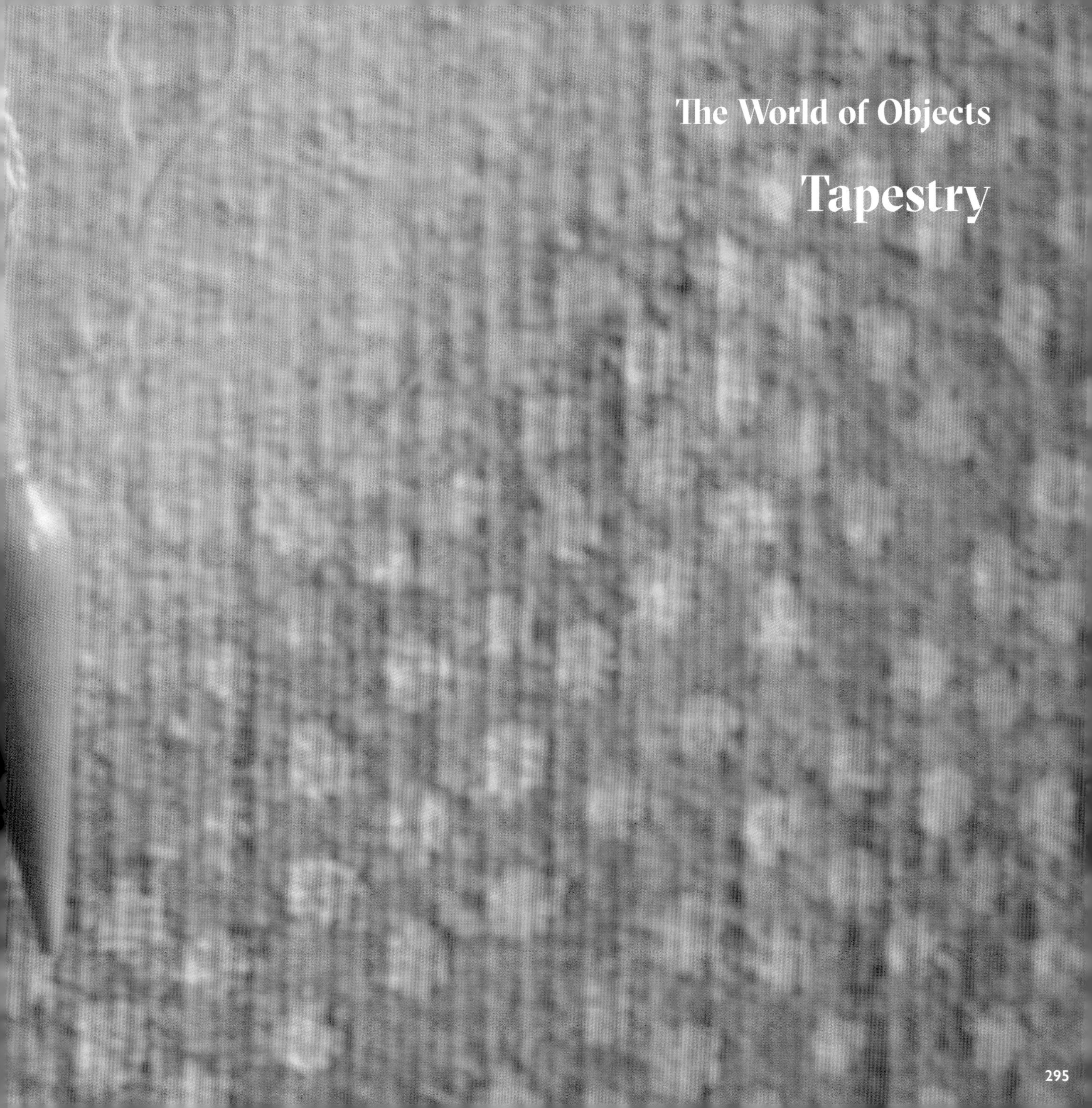

The World of Objects

# Tapestry

# JO BARKER (b.1963)

Jo Barker originally trained at Edinburgh College of Art, and works from her studio in Edinburgh whilst teaching as a senior lecturer at Glasgow School of Art. Her initial abstract designs are collaged together on computer from a combination of hand painted, drawn and inky marks. Colours are arranged in blocks, pools and smudges in overlapping layers. Employing this flowing way of designing is in complete contrast to the slow and intensive process of weaving. Wool, cotton and embroidery threads each have differing colour qualities. Combined, they offer a richness and depth of hue that continues to enchant, along with tapestry's unique sensibility of surface texture and material construction.

'A love of working with my hands: drawing, painting and making things; plus a long-term interest in colour are essentially at the heart of what I do. My compositions employ a range of marks, shapes and patterns which have evolved over a number of years, with recurring themes of ellipses, circles, halos; borders, edges and layers, creating a sense of movement and depth of field enhanced by reactions of particular colour combinations. The finished images are consciously abstract and ambiguous. I want to create a sense of something as opposed to an identifiable object or picture.' — Jo Barker

Public Collections include:
Victoria & Albert Museum, London
The House of Lords, London
National Museums Scotland, Edinburgh
Aberdeen City Art Gallery & Museums
Royal Victoria Infirmary, Newcastle
Scottish Executive, Edinburgh

Jo Barker's studio in Edinburgh, 2016

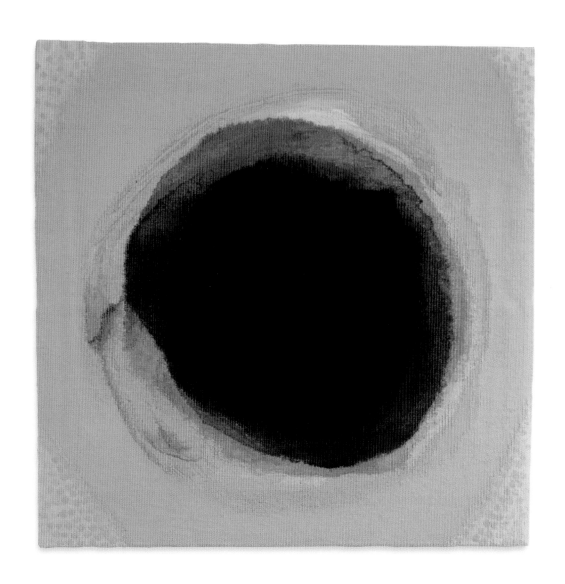

Cat.114, Jo Barker, Swirl, 2016, wool, cotton and embroidery threads, H75 x W75 cms

## SARA BRENNAN (b.1963)

Sara Brennan originally studied tapestry at Edinburgh College of Art. Her work is an unspoken response to the landscape. Using a refined and reduced approach to colour and form, her work takes two routes; weaving either from her drawings or reacting and responding in smaller works to yarns as they are placed directly next to each other. Sara Brennan obsessively explores the meetings that occur through the surface quality and by a manipulation and an exploitation of the line. She has exhibited internationally and her work is held in numerous public collections.

'I work from a series of drawings and paintings, often repeatedly exploring the translation of a surface or mark into tapestry. I also work as a direct response to the reaction and relationship between yarns, with a disciplined and restrained approach to colour, tone and form. Choosing each yarn is as important to me and the tapestry as making the original drawing. The yarn must work to help balance and convey the feel and mood. It is vital in the interpretation of the drawing, bringing the tapestry to life....' — Sara Brennan

Public Collections include:
Aberdeen City Art Gallery and Museums
HBOS Headquarters, Edinburgh
Scottish Parliament Building, Edinburgh
Shipley Art Gallery

Sara Brennan in her Edinburgh studio, 2017.
Photo: Norman MacBeath

Cat.115, Sara Brennan, Deep Forest with Old Green, 2015,
wool, cotton and linen, H70 x W56 cms. Photo: Shannon Tofts

Lise Bech's
willow harvest
in the Southern
Uplands

The World of Objects

# Willlow

## LISE BECH (b.1951)

Originally from Denmark, Lise Bech now lives and works in Fife, where she grows a wide range of willows (Salix species) for her basket making. In addition to her cultivated willow beds, the local landscape provides a rich source of other traditional basketry materials (heather, fieldrush, hairmoss) and more experimental fibre plants (birch, broom), which are occasionally used for embellishment.

Lise's initial interest and motivation in taking up basketry was her desire to be involved with the whole process of making beautiful and useful organic objects: from the growing and harvesting of the raw materials through to design and final execution of the piece – each step satisfying her love of and commitment to the natural world. Working exclusively with Scottish willow – much of it organically grown, tended and harvested (coppiced) by hand – she weaves traditional as well as contemporary pieces.

'I made my first basket whilst living in Northern Ireland under the expert tuition of the aptly named Ms Greenwood! When I moved to Scotland she gave me one hundred willow cuttings thus ensuring I would 'keep my hand in'. That was the start of my love affair with willow. Growing my own materials keeps me connected with the seasonal rhythms and has fostered a sense of pride and integrity with regards to the final product – homegrown, organic, carefully harvested and lovingly handmade in Scotland' — Lise Bech

Lise Bech in her studio. Photo: Tara Fisher

Cat.116, Lise Bech, The Southern Uplands Series, Goodbush Hill, 2016, Salix Lasiandra willow, H30 x W30 cms

### LIZZIE FAREY (b.1962)

Lizzie trained in fine art and stained glass before turning to basketry in 1991, learning the first steps from her sister-in-law in North Wales. She planted a field of willow cuttings and her passion for working with natural materials began. Always keen to try new approaches to this traditional craft, Lizzie gradually gained a strong reputation for her simple innovative forms, especially the spheres often decorated with catkins or pussy willow. Recent work has concentrated primarily on fine art wall pieces.

'I take my influences from the Galloway countryside where I live and work. I am surrounded by hills, lochs, larch and heather, the essence of which I try to recapture in my work. I grow my willow in nearby farmer's fields and collect ash and other materials from the hedgerows. My working life is governed by the cycle of nature. The work leads me and stimulates me at the same time. The pieces that I forge create a sense of spaciousness and take on a life of their own. I try to express the complex in as simple a way as possible – the natural materials often having a quiet and still effect on the viewer.' — Lizzie Farey, 2015

Lizzie Farey in her Galloway studio. Photo: Walter Neilson

Opposite: Lizzie Farey, When I Think of You, 2015, pussy willow and willow, D102 cms. Photo: Shannon Tofts

304

## JOE HOGAN (b.1953)

Joe Hogan is first and foremost a traditional basketmaker and fine artist. He has worked from his studio in Loch na Fooey in West Ireland since 1978. He grows his own willow, and harvests other naturally occurring materials such as wood, bark, larch, birch, bog myrtle twigs, willow twigs and catkins that he incorporates in his work. Joe Hogan is regarded as one of Ireland's master craftsmen and has gained a worldwide reputation for his work.

'I was drawn to basketmaking because willow growing provided an opportunity to live rurally and develop a real understanding for a particular place. Over the last 30 years I have found it a very satisfying occupation. I take some time each year to try new ideas and to make new designs but I also value repetition and the fluency it develops. You learn to be patient, to work in the present moment and to not prejudge the outcome. For the past 10 years or so I have become increasingly interested in making non-functional baskets, some of which involve the use of found pieces of wood. This work is prompted by a desire to develop a deeper connection to the natural world.' — Joe Hogan

Joe Hogan in his studio in Loch na Fooey, 2015. Photo: Peter Rowen, courtesy of Design & Crafts Council of Ireland

Opposite: Cat.117, Joe Hogan, Tall Vessel, 2015, willow, H80 x D50 cms

# Abbreviations

| | |
|---|---|
| ARA | Associate Member of the Royal Academy |
| ARBS | Associate of the Royal Society of British Sculptors |
| ARSA | Associate of The Royal Scottish Academy |
| CBE | Commander of the Most Excellent Order of the British Empire |
| DBE | Dame Commander of the Most Excellent Order of the British Empire |
| DHC | Doctor Honoris Causa |
| FRSE | Fellow of the Royal Society of Edinburgh |
| FRSA | Fellowship of the Royal Society of Arts |
| HRSA | Honorary Member of The Royal Scottish Academy |
| LG | London Group |
| MA (RCA) | Master of Art, Royal College of Art |
| MBE | Member of the Most Excellent Order of the British Empire |
| NEAC | New English Art Club |
| OBE | Officer of the Most Excellent Order of the British Empire |
| PPRSA | Past President of The Royal Scottish Academy |
| PPRSW | Past Present of the Royal Scottish Society of Painters in Watercolour |
| PPSSA | Past Present of the Scottish Society of Artists |
| PRSA | President of The Royal Scottish Academy |
| RA | Royal Academy |
| RBA | Royal Society of British Artists |
| RCA | Royal College of Art |
| RGI | Royal Glasgow Institute |
| RI | Royal Institute of Painters in Watercolour |
| RMS | Royal Society of Miniature Painters, Sculptors and Gravers |
| ROI | Royal Institute of Oil Painters |
| RP | Royal Society of Portrait Painters |
| RSA | Royal Scottish Academy |
| RSW | Royal Scottish Society of Painters in Watercolour |
| RWA | Royal West of England Academy |
| RWS | Royal Watercolour Society |
| SSA | Society of Scottish Artists |
| SSWA | Scottish Society of Women Artists |
| WIAC | Women's International Art Club |

# Museum and Institutional Patrons

Aberdeen Art Gallery and Museums

Aberystwyth University

Abbot Hall Art Gallery, Kendal

Arts Council of Northern Ireland, Belfast

Art Museum of Santa Barbara, California, USA

Australia National Gallery of Art, Sydney, Australia

Bury Art Museum and Sculpture Centre, Manchester

Carnegie Trust for the Universities of Scotland, Dunfermline

City Arts Centre, Edinburgh

Collins Art Gallery

Contemporary Arts Society, London

Crafts Council, London

Edinburgh College of Art

University of Edinburgh

The Fitzwilliam Museum, Cambridge

Glasgow Art Galleries and Museums

University of Glasgow

Gracefield Arts Centre, Dumfries

Graves Art Gallery, Sheffield

Heriot-Watt University, Edinburgh

Kettering Museum and Art Gallery

Kirkcaldy Galleries

Kunstmuseum, Dusseldorf, Germany

Laing Art Gallery, Newcastle

Lillie Art Gallery, Glasgow

London Crafts Council

Manchester City Art Gallery

McManus Galleries, Dundee

Middlesbrough Institute of Modern Art

National Gallery of Art, Sydney

National Galleries of Scotland

National Museums Northern Ireland, Belfast

National Museums Scotland, Edinburgh

National Museum of Victoria, Melbourne, Australia

National Museum Wales, Cardiff

National Portrait Gallery, London

Norwich Castle Museum and Art Gallery, Norfolk

Paisley Museum and Art Galleries

The Pearson Silver Collection, London

Perth Museum and Art Gallery

Public Art Gallery, Dunedin, New Zealand

Queen Margaret University, Edinburgh

Reading Museum

Ridderkerk District Council, Holland

Royal Edinburgh Hospital

Royal Ontario Museum, Toronto, Canada

University of St Andrews

St Anne's College, Oxford

Scottish Arts Council, Edinburgh

Scottish National Gallery of Modern Art

Scottish National Portrait Gallery

Museums Sheffield

University of Stirling

Tate Britain, London

Ulster Museum

Victoria & Albert Museum, London

University of Wales

The Watson Trust

Whitworth Art Gallery, Manchester

University of York

# Gallery Staff

Managing Director
Christina Jansen

Chairman
Will Whitehorn
Painting by Patrick Gibbs

Director
Guy Peploe

Director
Tommy Zyw

Finance Director
Innes Chalmers

Assistant Director
Breeshey Gray

Assistant Director
Alison McGill

Assistant Director
Kirsty Sumerling

Gallery Assistant
Elizabeth Jane Campbell

Accounts Assistant
Dominika Starzynska-Asare

Registrar, Administrator
and Art Technician
Wietske Veenhuis

*Modern Masters* exhibition catalogues 2013–2017.

# Buy from us

The Scottish Gallery offers a comprehensive and discreet service to those seeking advice on valuation or wishing to sell works of art. Sometimes it will be our advice to seek an appraisal with an auctioneer but these days the costs of conducting business at auction, particularly for a potential vendor, are such that today the Gallery option is much more attractive. Auction is like theatre and there can be bad as well as good days 'on the block.' How much better to have an entirely private and discreet arrangement with The Scottish Gallery who will take every consideration into account and charge considerably less for so doing. Do get in touch for a free appraisal and advice from Guy Peploe, Tommy Zyw and Christina Jansen, who between them have over sixty years of experience of the market to draw on.

# Sell with us

The Scottish Gallery would like to thank the many individuals
who have contributed to this publication, especially all the
artists, clients and institutions associated with The Gallery.

Particular thanks to the Macaulay family for allowing us to publish
*The Macaulay Children* by Joan Eardley, Stephen Dunn for his gallery staff
portraits and the Wilhelmina Barns-Graham Trust for archive images.

ISBN: 978-1-910267-59-2
Designed by Martin Baillie
Printed by J Thomson Colour Printers

Front cover: Joan Eardley, The Macaulay Children,
c.1957, oil on board, 60 x 37.5, 80, 37.5 cms

Inside covers: Archive catalogues and invitations

**THE**SCOTTISH**GALLERY**
CONTEMPORARY ART SINCE 1842

16 Dundas Street, Edinburgh, EH3 6HZ  |  +44 (0)131 558 1200
mail@scottish-gallery.co.uk  |  scottish-gallery.co.uk